£3.50

Planning at the crossroads

Planning
at the
crossroads

James Simmie
The Bartlett School of Planning
University College London

First published in 1993 by UCL Press

UCL Press Limited
University College London
Gower Street
London WC1E 6BT

The name of University College London (UCL) is a registered
trade mark used by UCL Press with the consent of the owner.

ISBN:
1-85728-024-5 HB
1-85728-025-3 PB

A CIP catalogue record for this book
is available from the British Library.

Typeset in Palatino.
Printed and bound by
Biddles Ltd, King's Lynn and Guildford, England.

To my family:

Linda, Imogen, Hamish

CONTENTS

PREFACE

Over 30 years ago Lewis Keeble (1961) published a small book called *Town planning at the crossroads*. In it he complained of the discrepancy between the sophistication of the administrative tools available to town planners and the lack of comprehensive and intelligent policies which they were being used to achieve.

I have adapted both his title and his criticism of British planning of so long ago because it seems to me that planning in Britain is at another major crossroads at the beginning of the 1990s. This latest watershed has been reached as a result of the conjuncture of at least three separate influences.

The first, and most remarked, is the combination of "right-wing" critiques of planning with a period of right-wing central government which has enthusiastically embraced the conclusions of many of these critiques. The resulting changes in both local government and planning during the 1980s are there for all to see. More change will certainly come during the 1990s.

The second, and much less discussed influence on the whole planning project, is the collapse of integrated economic, social and physical planning in Eastern Europe at the end of the 1980s. This has effectively discredited not only those regimes which attempted unsuccessfully to practice such planning but also the principles and practices of socialist styles of planning that have often informed British planning in the past. This makes a return to or renewal of such styles of planning a political non-starter, as the British Labour Party has found to its cost in losing four successive General Elections.

The third important element in where planning should attempt to go next is the long-term relative decline of the British economy as a whole. The current slump is more likely to prove a major milestone in this decline than the prelude to a significant long-term recovery without the intervention of planned industrial policy. In this respect British planning must take account of the sort of activities already practiced by its French and Japanese counterparts in seeking to enable and develop large-scale technopoles. It is essential to develop a new vision of the purposes of planning along these lines in order both to address one of Britain's main problems and to escape from the progressive curtailment of its very existence by central government and underfunded local authorities.

In order to move past planning's current crossroads in intelligent directions it is essential to know what the effects of past planning policies have been. The inspiration for this book came from initial attempts to summarize these effects which were largely frustrated by the general absence of systematic and adequate monitoring of the effects of British planning policies. This led to a longer-term project which sought to gather such monitoring material as was available, put it into some logical order and to compare it with similar material drawn from California. The reason for comparing it with California was primarily to address the problem of what effects can be attributed directly to planning. California before 1971, and even since that date, is used as an example of less or more relaxed planning regimes than the more consistently interventionist styles of Britain.

The results of these comparisons make up the core of this book. They seek to show what effects planning has had in the past on the transfer of rural to urban land uses, commuting patterns, land and house prices, economic growth and residential segregation. The conclusions drawn from this work are that planning in Britain needs to adopt new directions and policies to progress beyond its present crossroads during what little remains of the 20th century.

JAMES SIMMIE   LONDON   SEPTEMBER 1992

ACKNOWLEDGEMENTS

The work on which this book is based was funded by the Nuffield Foundation. Their willingness to fund planning research and the friendly encouragement of Patricia Williams are much appreciated.

The empirical material on California was collected under the guidance of Peter Hall by Robert Thompson at the Institute of Urban and Regional Studies, University of California, Berkeley. The corresponding material for Britain was assembled by Simon Olsberg and Christopher Tunnell at the Planning and Development Research Centre, University College London. I am grateful to all of them for their invaluable and helpful assistance.

I should also like to thank all those whose work I have used so freely in the text. A book such as this, which is based on secondary sources, clearly owes much to the inspiration and material provided by others. I hope that friends and colleagues will take citation of their work in the text as my personal thanks for its contribution to my own thoughts and this book.

Time to write the book was provided by a sabbatical term granted by the Bartlett Planning School at University College London. The active help provided by the School and colleagues to write, in these hard times for British universities, is essential and invaluable.

Last, but by no means least, I should like to thank my family for supporting the trials and tribulations which accompany book writing. The book is dedicated to them as a small consolation for a home-bound summer.

As usual, despite the very best endeavours of all those cited above, the warts and faults that remain are entirely the responsibility of the author.

JAMES SIMMIE   LONDON   SEPTEMBER 1992

xi

CHAPTER ONE
Introduction

Land-use planning in Britain is at one of its periodic crossroads. A growing number of separate internal and external forces for change have been gathering around planning during the 1980s. They have already led to significant change such as the abolition of the metropolitan counties and the introduction of urban development corporations, enterprise zones and unitary development plans. There are already suggestions for further change during the 1990s such as the reform of local government, the abolition of structure plans and the externalization of many existing planning functions from the hands of local planning authorities. There can be no doubt that further major changes will take place in planning during the next decade. There is, however, considerable doubt and argument about the purposes and nature of these changes.

The main argument in this book is that no debate about the future of planning can be based on informed argument without much clearer information on what it has done in the past. This does not mean taking past policy statements and inputs at their face value. What it does mean is that it is essential to know what the effects of past planning policies have been on the ground. The generic term for this activity is monitoring.

The paucity of genuine and significant monitoring of the effects of planning policies on the ground has always been an important weak link in British planning practice and research. The main predilection for most practitioners and researchers has been to focus on policy making

1

and inputs. There is very much less credible work on what the outputs of those policies have been.

The lack of adequate and up-to-date information on what planning does in this latter sense has hampered discussion of the activity. It has made it particularly susceptible to relatively unsubstantiated intellectual critiques. At the same time it has also hampered any rebuttal of those critiques and of central government actions based upon them. As a result changes have been taking place almost willy-nilly on the basis of arbitrary ideological whims. There is a need to know what planning has done in the past in order to discuss what it could do in the future on a more sound footing than this.

The factors and forces that have brought planning to its present cross-roads are:

(a) the end of its post-war vision and purposes;

(b) economic decline;

(c) intellectual critiques from right and left;

(d) central government changes to both planning and local government.

Statutory town planning was introduced in Britain in 1947 on the basis of the much discussed consensus of the need for post-war recon-struction to provide a motivating vision of the future for the masses involved in the war effort. This vision was the product of professional, political, industrial and agricultural elites. Its main objectives were to contain urban areas and to create self-contained and balanced communi-ties. It was based on the assumptions that urban sprawl should be con-trolled, the loss of good agricultural land prevented and future urban growth accommodated in self-contained new towns.

This vision has now faded for several reasons. The first is the obvious fact that post-war reconstruction has long since been completed. There is no war damage left to repair.

Secondly, the development of the European Community Common Agricultural Policy has produced vast surpluses of agricultural products. There is no longer any compelling reason to protect British farming and farmers for strategic or production reasons. Many of them are already being paid to set aside land from agricultural production. Much agricul-tural land in Britain is now surplus to any national requirements.

Thirdly, only a relatively small proportion of new urban growth has been accommodated in new and expanded towns. These have not been developed according to the original vision of large, city-scale groups but as traditional, small free-standing towns. Far from being self-contained, they have more often contributed to the growth of commuting.

Finally, and most importantly, British cities have only been contained physically but not functionally. Despite such draconian restrictions on their growth as Green Belts they have continued to expand beyond those belts. Not only has this contributed to increases in the volume, costs and time of commuting, but also to the protection of some interests at the cost of others. It has created a residential form of apartheid. Existing rural county property owners and the new service class have used Green Belts and other restrictive practices to raise the cost of access to their sub-urban environments. This has confined groups not able to meet these inflated costs or to move to the new and expanded towns to the older urban cores.

The remnants of the original vision and purpose of town planning could now be restated as the subsidization of unwanted agricultural activities and the maintenance of physical, residential apartheid. Meanwhile cities continue to de-urbanize and re-urbanize regardless of these major planning activities. Any consensus over such a vision has long since come to an end. It has become associated in the public mind with petty bureaucracy, nosey neighbours and timid, lowest-common-denominator design solutions. Such support as it now receives comes mainly from the special and partial interest groups whose fragmented ends it serves.

National, regional and urban economic decline has also brought planning to its present crossroads. Long-term economic decline in Britain has accelerated since the 1970s. The present slump is now the deepest since the Depression of the 1920s and 1930s. The effects of this decline are not distributed equally in space. Regions north of a line drawn from the Wash to the Severn have experienced the brunt of the decline of traditional heavy industry. The cores of older cities, where many of these industries were originally located, have also suffered.

The problems that this decline presents for post-war planning follow from the fact that planning has been primarily a reactive, regulative activity. With the notable exceptions of the new towns, planning does not itself produce development. What it does is to react to and regulate proposals for development brought forward by other, often private developers. This means that, particularly in times and places of economic slump, there is little that planning can actually do to produce development on the ground unless there is a demand for that development by other organizations. Localized injections of public investment in the relatively new urban development corporations are not of sufficient scale to invalidate this basic characteristic.

Planning in general has also been brought to a crossroads since the late 1970s by intellectual critiques, often associated with the political right, and, since the late 1980s, the collapse of integrated planning in Eastern Europe. The importance of these two challenges to traditional planning thought has not yet been recognized or accepted in Britain.

The intellectual critiques have often been brushed aside without full consideration of their force and validity. Yet this has been done while at the same time harking back to the now defunct post-war vision of the nature and purposes of planning. This vision contained some of the elements more generally present in the integrated command economies of Eastern Europe. The collapse of these economies, due largely to their inability to match the performance of even their poorest Western equivalents, should be prompting a radical re-assessment of planning thought. This has not, so far, been the case.

Despite the lack of a new vision, economic growth and a careful re-appraisal of the intellectual basis of planning, central government in Britain has been pressing ahead with major, radical changes to the system. More such changes and the reform of local government are planned for the immediate future. These changes have been driven through without much willing participation or input from planners themselves. This brings planners to the crossroads of the control of the content of planning and the profession itself.

If planners are unable to reformulate a new and clear vision of what planning should be about, it is difficult to participate in the arguments with a government that does have a strong view of the nature and content of the activity. Throughout the 1980s a strong central government was able to dictate many of the terms, conditions and professional content of planning. This is unlikely to change in the future without a radical re-appraisal by planners of what the profession should be seeking to do in the future. A return to the past is not an option.

The argument of this book is that the way forward for planning is not to espouse a new set of vague and untestable visions of the future. Artists impressions of tubes and domes, floating leisure parks and glass cars are irrelevant to the general credibility and acceptance of new forms of planning. Instead, it is necessary to step back in order to spring forward. The crucial step back involves taking the intellectual critiques of planning seriously and investigating whether there is any truth in them by analyzing what effects planning has produced in the past. Only when these have been fully documented will planning be in a position to spring forward on the basis of the knowledge of what policies are likely to produce which results in the future.

This general argument is developed in the following way. Chapter 2 sets out and analyzes the recent theoretical and practical critiques of planning. These are shown to be not exclusively right-wing. They emanate from the United States, Britain and Eastern Europe. The former Yugoslavia is used as an example of the problems associated with some of the most developed forms of integrated command planning.

Many of these arguments contrast planning with markets. There is an implicit assumption that these markets are competitive. Comparisons are therefore made between actual planning and hypothetical competitive markets. In practice markets are not usually perfectly competitive. This leads to the important paradox that planning has seldom replaced but has instead encouraged the development of imperfectly competitive and oligopolistic markets.

Chapter 3 examines the intellectual responses of planning to recent critiques. Planners are shown not to have taken them seriously enough and to hark back to an idealized version of the status quo ante. The case is made in detail for the need to step back and monitor the past effects of planning before springing forward to propose new activities. It is argued that in the past too much emphasis has been placed on the analysis of inputs to planning and not nearly enough attention devoted to its outputs on the ground.

Chapter 4 analyzes briefly the methodological problems of monitoring the specific effects of planning in the past. It is argued that there is a basic need to be able to disentangle the effects of planning from others that are present. In the future this could be done by setting up longitudinal studies of situations as they are now, introducing a planning policy and then observing what changes had been brought about by this policy at some relevant point in the future. This methodology cannot be used for the study of past policies.

In order to estimate the effects of past policies it is necessary to implement the comparative method. In this book it is used by taking California as a base line, with no containment policies before 1972, to compare with the gradual introduction of local growth management policies there after that date and the tough containment policies in the south of Britain as compared with the more relaxed policies in the north.

Chapters 5 and 6 detail the effects of planning in California and Britain. They are described systematically in terms of their effects on urban containment, suburbanization, land and housing prices, economic growth, and residential and social segregation. In each case the introduction of planning is estimated to have had unintended effects and to have benefited some groups while imposing costs on others.

In conclusion, Chapter 7 draws the comparison of the effects of planning together. It assesses the validity of the critiques of planning against these estimates of its effects. It concludes that in the future the long-standing appropriation of all private property rights in urban development should be reduced; that the policy of containment should be changed; that planning should be made more consistent; and that planning should support competitive development markets. These conclusions are directly related to the estimated effects of planning described in Chapters 5 and 6.

Taken together the arguments of the book lead to the conclusion that there are few directions that planning can take from its present crossroads. The "do nothing" direction leads to further unilateral central government action on the nature and content of planning. This is a direction which has already led to the erosion of independent professions and towards technical administration.

The "turn around and go back" direction leads towards decreasing relevance in the 1990s and continued decline in public support. It leads planning towards the kind of timid bureaucracy which has proved all too easy to merge or abolish altogether in the 1980s.

The active support of the "continued containment" direction heads straight into the teeth of contemporary intellectual and practical criticism. It serves only partial interests, maintains residential apartheid and does not generate much needed economic growth.

It is argued that to avoid these undesirable directions planning should be rethought in order to concentrate on major rather than minor issues, abandon the policy of urban containment, make better use of new information technology in decision making, and foster competitive development markets. The reasons for taking this direction are explained at length in the chapters that follow.

CHAPTER TWO
Theoretical critiques of planning

Introduction

This chapter discusses the important theoretical critiques of the concept of public planning in general and public land-use planning in particular. These have been developed in America, Britain and Eastern Europe (most accessibly in Yugoslavia). Among other things they have contributed to the intellectual bases of the regimes of Ronald Reagan and Margaret Thatcher; and help to explain the collapse of centralized planning in Eastern Europe. Land-use planning has been influenced both indirectly and directly by these critiques.

The chapter is divided into three sections. These sections examine the theoretical critiques of planning which have been developed in three different kinds of political economies. These are capitalist America, mixed Britain and the former, socialist Yugoslavia. The reason for choosing these three countries as the sources of critiques of planning is that they represent the spectrum of different planning regimes.

America and American critiques of planning are used to represent the views expressed in circumstances of what, in Britain, would be regarded as a relatively relaxed planning regime. The critiques emanating from that source are also associated with the ideology of neo-liberalism.

The former Yugoslavia is used as a relatively accessible example of the now mostly defunct European integrated command economies. These were based on the ideology of socialism.

These two polar examples can be used to compare with Britain which represents a relatively tough planning regime but one confined primarily to issues of land-use.

Bearing in mind the differences in political economy and ideology between these three examples, it is surprising how similar are the critiques of planning that emanate from them. These are outlined in the following three sections which are:

(a) American critiques of planning;
(b) British critiques of planning;
(c) Yugoslavian critiques of planning.

American critiques of planning

A loosely grouped collection of critiques of planning has been labelled "new right". This label is not altogether justified as many of the critics have either been associated with the centre left in British politics or socialist as opposed to communist groups in Eastern Europe. The problem with many of these latter critics is that their work has either been suppressed or has not been accessible in English translations. What they do often have in common, however, are intellectual backgrounds in philosophy or economics. It might, therefore, be more accurate to describe them as philosophical and economic critiques. This label is more helpful in understanding their characteristics, which will be discussed below.

Among the most accessible and, partly for this reason, therefore best known conceptual critiques of planning are those of philosophers and economists living in America. Their original intentions were to combat a perceived intellectual drift towards socialist inspired ideas of equality and economic planning by theorizing the superiority of market forces in generating economic growth. The most prominent among them are Friedrich von Hayek and Milton Friedman.

In a series of publications, von Hayek (1944, 1960, 1982) argued that the market economy is the best way to ensure prosperity, the rule of law and liberty. His basis for this argument is that a central authority cannot command the information which would be necessary for it to substitute its judgement for the dispersed information and preferences of a multitude of firms and individuals. Planning is therefore less capable and efficient than markets.

In a further two books, Friedman (1962, Friedman & Friedman, 1980) also argued that prosperity and therefore optimum economic growth is best achieved by markets rather than planning. The central thrust of both these writers is that markets do better and more rationally what planning seeks to do. We should therefore prefer markets to planning.

These ideas influenced the British Conservative Party elite while in opposition under Margaret Thatcher during the 1970s. Andy Thornley (1991: Ch. 5) describes how they came to be incorporated in critiques of physical planning during successive Conservative administrations in the 1980s. He notes how this attack was heralded by the publication of *A bibliography of freedom* in 1980 by Sir Keith Joseph's right-wing Centre for Policy Studies. This bibliography has a short section of 16 references on "Urban policy". Half of these are American books showing the potentially strong influence of transatlantic ideas on the attitudes of the Conservative government elite to British planning.

Seminal American books in this bibliography include Jane Jacobs's *The death and life of great American cities* (1965) and *The economy of cities* (1970); Edward Banfield's *Unheavenly city revisited* (1974); and Bernard Siegan's *Land-use without zoning* (1972) and *Other people's property* (1976). Taken together their analyses of American planning practices and effects provide the bases of a damning critique of collectivist-style city planning in America.

Jane Jacobs argues that such planning has failed to stem the decay of some American cities and, worse still, has even contributed to their economic decline. She maintains that contemporary planners have had no new major ideas since the days of Ebeneezer Howard and Le Corbusier. They therefore continue to follow the old ideas of self-containment, the inward looking neighbourhood, decentralization, grass instead of streets, control of commercial activity and the wish to sort out uses into separate land-use zones. The reasons that she gives for the adoption of these principles echo von Hayek. They are that planners are unable to understand and cope with the complexity of city life. As a result of this

10

inability planners fall back on unsubstantiated and meaningless simplifications.

Edward Banfield goes further and argues that because of the characteristics of man and society it is just not possible to solve serious problems by rational management. He distinguishes between problems which are issues of comfort, convenience, amenity and business advantage and those which threaten the essential welfare of society. While the latter are truly "serious" problems, the former are not. He accuses planners of devoting most of their attention to the issues of comfort, convenience, amenity and business advantage. He regards this whole effort as misplaced because these problems are either unimportant, will take care of themselves, or will be made worse by planning. His "general message . . . is that government intervention wastes money and time on schemes that are geared to insignificant problems that will take care of themselves anyway or on people who can never be helped until their attitudes change" (Thornley 1991: 99). Governments should not, in Banfield's view, interfere in economic growth, demographic change and lower-class aspirations for improved status.

Bernard Siegan criticizes planning for its lack of rationality and for succumbing to pluralist political pressures. In another echo of von Hayek he also says that the issues with which planners deal are impossibly complex when they come to assess the correct use for plots of land. He argues that there is no rational way of doing this and therefore planning must be subjective. It lacks the standards and measuring abilities of a scientific discipline. As a result, planners are subject to the political pressures of those who employ them. Land-use regulations are therefore more a tool of politics than of planning. The effects of different and often conflicting political pressures on planning are that its outcomes, or effects, are totally unpredictable and irrational.

Siegan contrasts planning with the market. In the land market developers have to risk money and their own future livelihood. As a result, they take great care to understand the needs of consumers. They satisfy consumers and thereby make profits. Because, according to Siegan, the unfettered working of land markets produces these more desirable results than planning, most government powers over land-uses should be abolished. Using the city of Houston as an example, he advocates the removal of all zoning regulations in America.

British critiques of planning

British references cited in the *Bibliography of freedom* (1980) include an article in *New Society* called "Non-plan: an experiment in freedom" by Banham et al. (1969); and work produced in the Cambridge Department of Land Economy notably by Denman (1980), *Land in a free society* and Pearce et al. (1978), *Land, planning and the market*; also the work of the Institute of Economic Affairs notably in Walters et al. (1974), *Government and the land*; and the Adam Smith Institute's *Omega Report; local government policy* (1983).

The article by Banham et al. argued that the purpose of planning had been lost and that society would be better without it. They suggested the idea which is credited with the inspiration of the policy of enterprise zones. This idea consisted in setting up zones in which planning was abolished altogether and people were given back their individual freedom of action. Although this is essentially a free market proposal, it is by no means accurate to characterize its authors as right-wing. Some of them have been Fabians and may be located somewhere in the centre left of British politics.

Denman argues that planning now lacks a clearly defined purpose. While this was initially to reconstruct war damaged Britain, this is no longer relevant and has not been superseded by newer and more contemporary purposes. Despite this the planning system has been altered piecemeal since the Second World War, and the lack of a clear guiding purpose has led to a hotchpotch of a system. Denman also echoes von Hayek when he argues that the pursuit of social equality in both market and collective economies has and will prove an unobtainable chimera. He is particularly concerned that the pursuit of such vague concepts undermines private property rights. This is because, according to Denman, the government's primary purpose is to protect individual property rights.

Pearce et al. (1978), argue that planning ignores the positive attributes of market processes and interferes in them unnecessarily. They cite examples of paternalistic developments such as Bournville, Saltaire and Port Sunlight and speculative developments such as Westminster, Bloomsbury and Bath in support of this contention. They go on to argue that where such developments arise without planning, then the costs of the planning system itself are an unnecessary drag on economic growth. In such circumstances it is preferable to let markets operate even if they are inefficient, if the costs of this inefficiency are less than those of planning interventions.

The views of von Hayek are echoed yet again when Pearce et al. argue that planning cannot deal with the complexity of interdependencies relating to the uses of urban land. They assert that market processes automatically take account of these complex interactions. Along with Banfield (1974) they also argue that some injustices have to be accepted because the tools available to planners can never be sophisticated enough to deal with them.

Walters et al. develop an additional critique of planning. This postulates that planning restricts the supply of land for building. This in turn pushes up the price of land and hence the prices of buildings and housing on it. If there was no planning, more building land would be available and everyone would benefit from cheaper housing. This argument applies particularly to Green Belt land where planning restrictions are most severe and demand is high.

A final criticism from Walters et al. again follows the arguments of von Hayek and Friedman. They argue that government planning interventions create a separate power structure. This displaces some of the conflicts of markets into the realm of politics. The private gains resulting from the granting of planning permissions are potentially so great that this opens up the system to possibilities of corruption. "Planning creates conditions in which each property-owner has an enormous incentive to wangle, cajole, threaten, use special influence and ultimately to bribe, and where politicians and civil servants have immense power and temptation placed in their hands" (Walters et al. 1974: 5).

The Adam Smith Institute's *Omega Report* on local government policy covers finance, planning and housing. The section on planning argues that planning promotes community values in opposition to the pursuit of personal profit and that this is not compatible with a free society. British planning denies the owners of property the automatic right to develop their property to their own best advantage. This curtails their individual freedom. In addition, it is argued that the general public as consumers have had no control over planning. Instead control has been exercised by the "planning class" or organized pressure groups.

A second criticism is that the planning process is unpredictable. This is because, first, its aims are not clear and are therefore open to wide interpretation. Secondly, because planners have a large amount of administrative discretion there is too much variation in decisions as between one place and another and between one planner and another. As a result planners impose arbitrary decisions in the name of the "community interest". These decisions, however, impose costs on those very same communities. Firstly there are the costs of preventing wealth creating activities. Secondly, costs are generated as a result of delays and lengthy appeals. Thirdly, costs are increased by the unnecessarily high standards imposed on densities and materials by planners.

The third criticism is that planners have not achieved their community aims despite the imposition of extra costs to the market. The drab uniformity of much British housing and the poor quality of public authority housing estates are given as evidence of this problem.

The *Omega Report* concludes that, on the bases of these criticisms, planners should stop trying to impose spurious community values through the control of land-uses. It suggests experiments with the use of four other control mechanisms: economic forces; the laws of nuisance; central regulation; and private institutional controls.

Yugoslavian critiques of planning

These critiques of public planning in America and Britain are reasonably well known partly because of their accessibility in English. Discussions of planning in the Eastern Europe of the 1980s are few and far between. This is partly because of the limited possibilities for critiques of the old regimes there and partly because of the barrier of language.

Possibly the best known analyses of Eastern European public planning by an East European are those of conditions in Hungary by Ivan Szelenyi (e.g. 1978). These have been published in English after he left that country. One of his main contentions was that market capitalism had been entirely replaced by an authoritarian state and bureaucracy in Eastern Europe. That being so, public planning became the dominant form of decision making.

Despite the relative separation of intellectual debates about planning between West and East Europe during the post-war period, it is significant to find similar critiques of public planning developing in both political areas. Among the most accessible of these are those developed in what used to be Yugoslavia. Some of this local work has been brought together by Simmie & Dekleva (1991).

Yugoslavia was both typical and unique in Eastern Europe. It was typical in being a single party, communist state. It was unique in developing the concept and practice of self-management. At first sight this appears to be the antithesis of other East European systems. The constitutional changes of 1974, together with the Associated Labour Act of 1976, seemed to establish a decentralized and plural system of industrial, political, territorial and interest-delegated decision making.

Public services and infrastructure were provided by self-management interest communities. These were "voluntary" combinations of self-managed producer enterprises and local communities. Delegates from the latter pursued local collective consumption interests.

However, Janez Smidovnik (1991) argues that the self-management of enterprises has suffered from four main problems. First, there was the problem of ownership. The "social ownership" of enterprises in effect came to mean that no property interests were represented in planning. The second problem followed from the first. Where the state, directors and workers in enterprises did not accept ownership responsibilities there was a tendency for them all to use the enterprise for their own different ends. The third problem was that under this system it was very difficult to make authoritative decisions in the light of any independent economic or managerial assessment of what they should be for any particular enterprise *per se*. The fourth problem identified by Janez Smidovnik is the attempt to solve economic problems mainly within the political and organizational confines of the commune. The commune proved to be too small a geographic unit within which to plan economic activities.

Smidovnik (1991) also criticizes the public planning and provision of collectively consumed services and goods such as social services and infrastructure. The institutional vehicles for achieving these ends were self-management interest communities. They proved more or less incapable of providing adequate social services and infrastructure on their own and were consequently abolished.

Zagorka Golubovic (1991) argues that genuine self-government is incompatible with one-party Marxist states. Real self-government requires a developed civil society separate and independent from the state. In some ways this echoes von Hayek's argument that activities should be separated from the state and conducted in free markets as the best way to ensure prosperity, the rule of law and liberty.

Joze Mencinger (1991) argues that poor economic performance, as much as anything else, led to the reform programme launched in 1988. During the 1960-80 period the increase of Gross National Product (GNP) per unit of investment in the planned Yugoslavian economy was only 70 per cent of the corresponding increase in comparable market economies of southern Europe (Bajt 1987). Both Mencinger (1991) and Bogomir Kovac (1991) show how publicly planned, collective, socialist solutions to running the Yugoslavian economy and its individual enterprises/associations have foundered upon poor economic performance. The objectives of the reforms were therefore no less than to create new integral product, labour and capital markets.

Unlike Banfield's (1974) critique of American planning, few could accuse East European planners of not being directly concerned with the major issue of social equality. But, Barbara Verlic-Dekleva (1991) points out that although human and social equality were major objectives of the post-war transformation of Yugoslavia, they have not been achieved in practice. Yugoslavian social policy has not been a means to reduce social inequalities. After nearly half a century of the communist experiment major inequalities persist between regions, workers, those without work and those confined to the "grey" economy.

Pavel Gantar & Srna Mandic (1991) examine the effects of communist

16

housing policies and their contribution to social equality. Shortages in housing supply have persisted. The formal construction sector is unable to supply enough housing. Workers have therefore been left to build their own accommodation. A large, informal self-build sector has developed in most major cities. Major housing inequalities have therefore emerged between those in the more desirable social housing and those in self-build accommodation.

In urban areas, Ognjen Caldarovic (1991) shows that inequalities in location are added to those of housing quality to produce further social inequality in cities. He reports research findings which show that different social status groups were in possession of different housing rights and that, in Zagreb, higher social status groups were found concentrated disproportionately in central areas while workers were more often concentrated on the periphery.

Examples such as these drawn from Eastern Europe show how far the practice of integrated planning differed from the theory. As one end of a continuum running from no planning to integrated command planning it shows, in an extreme form, the limitations of traditional socialist forms of planning. Such limitations need to be avoided in any future revisions of land-use planning in Britain.

Conclusions

The collective thrust of these American, British and Yugoslavian evaluations of public economic, social and land-use planning is that much of it does not appear to have achieved its formal objectives. The corollary is that markets could do better without the direct costs imposed by planning administrations.

Firstly, there is the general proposition that public planning systems have serious faults and that the processes of control should be shifted away from those systems and their political context and into the market and legal systems.

Secondly, it is argued that the real problems of cities arise from poverty. This is beyond the scope and remit of land-use planning. Planners

17

are therefore irrelevant to the solution of these problems and have actually made them worse by their interference. As in Yugoslavia, even where there was an attempt to integrate the different kinds of public planning, social and housing policies have not overcome the problems arising from poverty.

Thirdly, the main problem created by planning is that it interferes with the proper working of the market. Markets and not planners are the only mechanisms that can deal with the complexities of cities.

Fourthly, planning has reduced wealth creation. This is a cost of planning that has to be borne by society. It is argued that "a dynamic and prosperous city economy requires inefficiency in its structure and land-use and the rational pursuit of order by planners and others will kill off the potential economic growth sector, innovation and experimentation" (Thornley 1991: 117). Certainly, public economic planning in Yugoslavia seems to have reduced economic growth to 70 per cent of that in comparable southern European economies such as that of Greece.

Fifthly, there is some criticism of the strong relationships between planning and politics. This is said to provide the potential for various forms of corruption. It has also allowed some well organized pressure groups to use the planning system for their own particular ends. This is true in both East and West. In Yugoslavia the party and business elites have been able to use the housing and planning systems to obtain access to the highest quality and cheapest accommodation in the best urban locations.

Sixthly, there is also the theme that planners impose their own values on communities. This is often done to the detriment of the poorer classes. Vague and meaningless concepts such as "social equality", "wealth distribution" and "environmental protection" are used to impose these values and undermine private property rights. This is again clearest in the most planned case, that of Yugoslavia, where social equality formed a key element in planning ideology but was evident more in the breach than in the practice.

Finally, there is the problem of the costs generated by the planning system itself. Delays in the planning process push up developers' costs. Restrictions in the supply of land cause higher land and house prices. All these costs are attached to the planning system as opposed to markets. Generally, the solutions proposed to solve these problems involve some dismantling of the planning system. This is also most noticeable in Eastern Europe where the dash to dismantle planning has been most marked.

Most of the critics in this group, however, do not suggest the abolition of public planning altogether. They are almost all agreed that it has an important rôle to play in relation to market externalities. These externality effects are those created unintentionally or beyond the control of prices in a given market. Air pollution, for example, is created as a by-product of profitable production and the use of internal combustion engines in vehicles. Free markets do not put prices on this pollution so it is likely to continue, unless governments step in on the basis of a plan to reduce or prevent it. There are a whole range of what are called "pure and impure public goods and services" such as this which only public action by governments on the basis of plans can cure, supply or charge a price for. The systematic analysis of such goods and services is known as welfare economics. This will be discussed at greater length in the concluding chapter of this book.

Western critics of public planning are also mostly agreed that it should be minimal. In a more general extension of the enterprise zone idea they argue that planning should be restricted to limited types of area such as Areas of Outstanding Natural Beauty (AONBs). Market forces should be allowed full reign in the majority of areas.

A third proposition is that such public planning as remains should be made more consistent by taking it out of local politics and into the realm of law. The laws of nuisance and restrictive covenants are mentioned as the main vehicles for accomplishing this change. In Eastern Europe this is more problematic because first of all civil society has to be disentangled and separated from the state. Secondly, a whole new and independent legal system has to be established before it could begin to adjudicate in such matters as land-use conflicts.

Fourthly, it is suggested that planning should continue to provide infrastructure for development. The recent British privatization of basic utilities such as electricity and water, and (at the time of writing) the impending privatization of British Rail, mean, however, that the public provision of infrastructure is declining. Such utilities can be privatized because they become private instead of public monopolies. They can then charge consumers more or less what they like and thus maintain high profits even in times of economic slump.

Finally, there are suggestions that planning should provide an information and prediction service to help private sector firms and developers plan their future private activities. There are many private companies that provide such services at the moment, albeit at considerable cost. In the light of the predilection for market solutions, however, there does not seem to be much of an argument for public planning institutions effectively to subsidize the information needs of private producers.

One final theoretical consideration should be borne in mind while following the analyses in this book. That is, how far the intellectual critiques of Western planning and the more-or-less universal collapse of planned regimes in Eastern Europe strike at the very heart of socialist and Marxist-inspired planning theory. The Eastern European experience in particular has been one of the longest experiments in public planning ever tried. At the end of the day the experiment appears to have failed. This indicates that there are probably serious flaws in the original ideas themselves as well as in their execution in practice.

CHAPTER THREE
The planning response

Introduction

British planning theorists and practitioners have tended to adopt a lofty and disdainful attitude towards the critiques outlined in Chapter 2. They have often been brushed aside as temporary aberrations in the path of continuing post-war planning. Those who have attempted to respond to the critiques fall roughly into two main groups. The first group argue that post-war British planning principles and practice were reasonably sound. This leads to the conclusion that the theoretical critiques of these principles have been unreasonable and that revised versions should be re-established after the demise of Thatcherism. The views of this group are summarized in the first section of this chapter.

The second section argues that the critiques of planning should be taken more seriously because changes in planning in Britain during the 1980s and 1990s represent a sea-change in the theory and practice of planning and not just a temporary aberration. Furthermore, effective argument with these changes must rest on empirical evidence of what the effects of past planning policies have been. This leads to the argument the results of planning should be monitored effectively and that this has not usually happened in the past. This is the main reason why it has been so difficult to defend post-war planning practice against its critics. Monitoring should be a key and integral part of planning theory and practice.

The lack of adequate systematic monitoring in the past is illustrated in the third section. There the very few British monitoring studies are outlined. These are divided into those dealing with the physical effects of land-use planning and those assessing their economic and social consequences.

Finally, in a fourth section, the lack of consistent longitudinal monitoring of the effects of planning over time leads to a discussion of the methods needed to overcome this problem which are used in this book. Here it is argued that, because of the lack of continuous monitoring of planning in the past, now the only way to disentangle and pick out the specific effects of past planning from those of other public policies and private actions is to use the comparative method. Thus, because of the previous lack of monitoring, it is now necessary to compare the effects on land-uses of different levels of planning regime in order to analyze what differences the presence or absence of specific planning policies have made to those uses and their consequences.

The necessary use of the comparative method leads to the case studies of different planning regimes used to illustrate the effects of planning in this book. California before the 1970s is used as the base line from which to compare the effects of the introduction of planning. The reason for this is that up to that time California had no policies for urban containment. This has been a primary characteristic of the British planning system. The no containment era in California is compared with the effects of the development of local growth management policies. These in turn are compared with relaxed containment in the north of England and with tough containment policies in the south.

Status quo planning responses

The main response in Britain to the theoretical critiques of planning during the 1960s and 1970s and the political action, partly based on those critiques, in the 1980s, has been either to ignore them altogether or to advocate a return to the status quo ante. This has not been a particularly effective response.

One group of status quo theorists has defined the concept of what planners do to the extremely narrow idea of what they do, on a daily basis, in their offices. Basing their work on the highly abstract sociology of Habermas (1984), they seek to confine the study of what planners do to the relatively insignificant issue of the interpretation of their discussions with others during the course of their work. Prominent among such status quo planning theorists are Forester (1987), and Healy (1992).

This approach has been rightly criticized by, for example, Eric Reade (1987) and Chris Paris (1982) as, first, a defence mechanism against the kind of unfavourable evidence produced by social science researchers and political attacks from the new right; and, secondly, for ignoring what actually happens on the ground as a result of planning actions. It also ignores the discussions inspired by the work of Rex & Moore (1967) and Pahl (1970) on urban managers/gatekeepers, on the relative significance of groups such as planners in producing important urban effects. The consensus resulting from these discussions was that it was a mistake to concentrate on the "middle dogs" of the urban power structure while ignoring those at the top who actually laid down policy.

One conclusion that can be drawn from these criticisms of status quo planners is that the effects of planning must be seen as the results of the planning system as a whole. They are not only or even significantly produced by local, public planning authority bureaucrats working in their local town halls. Any significant effects of planning are much more likely to be the result of the operation of the system as a whole which, in Britain at least, involves the actions of the Secretary of State, his department, the results of appeals, local politicians and bureaucrats together with those interests, organizations and groups with which they negotiate and bargain over planning policies and decisions.

A more relevant group of status quo ante British planning theorists is represented in the works of, for example, Brindley et al. (1989), *Remaking planning* and Thornley (1991) *Urban planning under Thatcherism*. This work analyzes the movement of British public planning towards market variations during the 1980s. This movement was at least partly inspired by the critiques of old-style planning outlined in Chapter 2.

Brindley et al. conclude that the problems of market-led planning are "its social divisiveness, its lack of accountability, its short-termism and its inherent instability" (1989: 183). Having reached these conclusions, however, they then go on to advocate a return to something like the status quo ante. They accord first priority to the re-statement (emphasis added) of the case for long-term strategic planning. Secondly, they advocate the re-discovery of community values such as cooperation and fraternity. Both of these ideas were part of the post-war collectivist planning project.

Thornley argues that the weaknesses of Thatcherite market planning are its failure to consider inefficiencies of markets, its inability to deal satisfactorily with environmental issues and its attack on (local) democracy. He argues that markets lack morality and that this, together with the decline of local democracy, could be corrected by a re-turn to neighbourly and community values.

These brief analyses of somewhat idealized past planning practices tend to ignore three fundamental problems. The first is that, as Reade (1987) has argued, the idea of community failed to provide the basis for consistent and adequate planning practice during the heydays of post-war British planning. The scale of the problem of, for example, poverty was always much greater than the capabilities of planned and balanced communities to ameliorate. Secondly, much the same could be said about traditional post-war regional policy. In their seminal evaluation of the effects of regional policy Moore et al. (1986) conclude that to have solved the regional problem during the 1970s, policies would have had to have been three times more effective than they actually were. Finally, it is argued here that sea-changes have taken place during the 1980s both in economic structures and planning possibilities that make a return to previous forms of planning next to impossible. These changes will be discussed in more detail in the concluding chapter of this book.

One issue raised by Thornley (1991) does present some interesting possibilities for future planning policies. This is the question of the environment. Here it may be remembered that, in Britain, public health legislation was the forerunner of statutory town planning. The Public Health Act of 1875 is usually regarded as the first effective piece of legislation affecting town planning in this country. Environmental issues have many of the same characteristics as public health issues. First, they affect most people regardless of wealth, income and social class. Secondly, they often result from the unfettered operation of private markets and cannot be dealt with by individual private actions on their own. Thirdly, they fall into the category of public goods and are therefore susceptible to theoretical analysis on the basis of welfare economics. Finally, and importantly from the main argument of this book, many of the effects of public policies concerned with them can be measured empirically.

Nevertheless, these responses to the critiques of planning do not offer any empirical evidence on what the physical and consequential economic and social effects of planning have been. They are primarily concerned with various levels of policy inputs to and political debates surrounding planning in Britain during the 1980s. Their criticisms of the critics are not supported by evidence of the results of past planning. Without such evidence debates on or rebuttals of critiques of planning are primarily a matter of opinion. During the 1980s the opinions of the so called "new right" often prevailed. Among the reasons for this was the lack of any hard information about the effects of past planning policies which could be used in evidence against them.

The need for monitoring

The relative inability of planning theorists and practitioners to respond effectively to the intellectual critiques outlined in Chapter 2 leads directly to the main question posed in this book. This question is, "What are the effects or outcomes of land-use planning?" Answers to this seminal question provide the essential first step in discussions about the merits of different policies.

At first glance this might seem to be a question to which there are already plenty of adequate answers. Planners themselves tell us that what they do is to create such things as good home environments, provide for leisure and tourism, conserve buildings, the countryside and landscape, improve the natural and built environments, create more jobs and better places to work, make sure that developments are well served by transport systems, encourage interesting places to shop and visit, and manage mineral resources. These are indeed what the Royal Town Planning Institute (RTPI) said were the positive benefits of planning in a pamphlet to mark the institute's 75th anniversary in 1989.

But words such as "good", "improve", "better", "well" and "interesting" are all used on the basis of implicit rather than explicit ideas and value judgements about what actually constitutes such things as a "good home environment" or "better places to work". In order for external observers of planning practices to know whether any of these desirable ends have really been achieved, detailed definitions of them are required together with evidence of what planning has contributed in practice to their realization on the ground.

Such definitions and empirical evidence have been conspicuous by their absence in the past. It is more usually the case that the alleged results of planning are not substantiated by empirical evidence confirming that these are actually the outcomes of planning. Even where they can be shown to arise, it is difficult to ascertain for certain whether they are effects of planning, the operation of other agencies or even the outcome of market forces. In the absence of such empirical support it is not even known whether these phenomena come to exist at all, far less whether they have arisen as a direct result of the actions of any planners or planning system!

At a general level it is known that wide-ranging and linked social, economic and land-use planning failed to produce effects and outcomes which could sustain the collectivist regimes of Eastern Europe (e.g. Simmie & Dekleva 1991). This collapse of planning in Eastern Europe has very significant theoretical and practical implications for planning in the advanced Western democracies.

But at a detailed level Western planning has been almost silent on what its effects have been. This has left a limited knowledge base with which to discuss such effects intelligently. The key concept that could lead to the development of such knowledge is that of "monitoring". Monitoring is the process of discovering what the effects of planning policies have been. Despite the key significance of monitoring, the standard British textbooks on planning either do not mention monitoring at all (Ratcliffe 1974, Bruton & Nicholson 1987, Cullingworth 1985) or make only passing and inconsistent references to it (Healy 1983).

This book is, therefore, primarily concerned with redirecting the attention of planning theory and practice to the question of monitoring what planning does. In practice this means specifying what the outcomes of carefully defined land-use planning policies are within defined geographic aggregates. It is primarily concerned with the missing link in most planning activities - accurate, long-term monitoring of what the measurable effects of planning have been.

The case for concentrating on the effects of planning is well made by Reade (1987). He argues that the justification for government activities must be couched in terms of the effects produced by those activities. The process that should identify those effects is monitoring. Monitoring is usually included in the commonly used five-stage model of the land-use planning process. The stages of this model are adapted from that propounded by Patrick Geddes (1915) in *Cities in evolution: an introduction to the town planning movement and to the study of civics*. The first three stages of Geddes' model were:

(a) survey;

(b) analysis;

(c) plan;

to which were added, during the 1960s:

(d) monitor;

(e) review.

The problem with this model, identified by Reade (1987) is that most plans have conflated and confused the processes of monitor and review.

Kingston (1981) reviewed all the published monitoring documents of all the British structure planning authorities. He attempted to find out how these documents distinguished between monitor and review. His conclusion was that they invariably did not do so. He goes on to identify the original definitions of these two concepts. These are:

(a) Monitor Discovering the effects of policies which have been put into effect;

(b) Review Examining the emerging political and economic situation with a view to deciding whether these existing policies should be changed.

He concludes that what has tended to happen in practice is that monitoring has been conflated with review. This has excluded the discovery of the effects of past policies.

Reade (1987) argues that the general exclusion of effective monitoring from British land-use planning has left a crucial theoretical gap in planners' practical abilities to develop new or improved policy proposals. This gap arises because of their inability to anticipate policy outcomes on the basis of known effects of previous policies.

It is argued here that such knowledge is a crucial first step in the development of planning theory and research. We cannot begin to hypothesize the possible effects and outcomes of different proposed planning policies without knowing, in some detail, what the effects of past policies have been. The credible studies that have attempted to do this in the past stand out because of their limited number. Those studies will now be summarized briefly.

Past studies of British planning

Inputs

Past studies of the effects of British planning can be divided into two main categories. These are studies of policy inputs, which are the predominant type, and evaluations of policy outputs, which are a limited minority.

The studies of policy inputs need not detain the narrative here for long. Strictly speaking they do not deal with monitoring the effects of planning and are not, therefore, central to the main theme of this book. They do, however, bear upon one of the main theoretical critiques of planning raised in Chapter 2, that planning is politics and is therefore susceptible to political manipulation and misuse. This manipulation at the policy-making and input stage is clearly likely to have significant results in terms of policy outputs and effects.

An important line of research into how different organizations and groups have manipulated planning policy can be found in the British literature. It starts in the 1970s with Ferris (1972) who showed how middle-class residents in Islington, London, were able to influence local planning policy to free themselves from through traffic while subjecting working-class residents living nearby to much increased traffic.

Lee et al. (1974) showed how the county of Cheshire, outside Manchester, was able to prevent Manchester from acquiring land outside its boundaries to build public housing for its working-class residents. It was also able to use the planning system to prevent expansion in small industrial areas and exclusive suburbs which also hindered the housing of Manchester's working class.

Elkin (1974) analyzed the respective rôles of the London Borough of Chelsea and the now defunct Greater London Council. He showed how developers were able to extract huge concessions from the local planning authorities in return for small concessions on their part.

Saunders (1979) studied the London Borough of Croydon. Among other things, he showed how powerful some local landed interests were in moulding local planning policies to their own interests.

Simmie (1981) analyzed planning policy in Oxford over a long period from the Second World War to the end of the 1970s. He demonstrated how planning policies were shaped by the internal, corporatist, participation of the university and local business interests in both their making and implementation. Some policies were also influenced by the organized local labour movement.

Simmie (1986) also shows how, at the national level, the House Builders' Federation has been able to manipulate the Department of the Environment's policy on housing land availability. He shows how they were able to insist that they were involved with local planning authorities to ensure that a five-year supply of building land on bigger sites became available in the home county structure plans.

Finally, Brindley et al. (1989) show both the variety of styles of influence over the planning system and the overall problem of drawing consistent conclusions from these studies. They identify six types of planning style to be found in different areas in Britain during the 1980s. These are identified in Figure 3.1. On the one hand they found examples of the continuation of post-war planning styles involving public regulation and investment. To this had been added popular planning which emerged to increase public inputs into planning policies during

29

the 1970s. On the other hand, they argued that market-led planning is becoming the dominant form of planning in Britain. This takes the form, in different types of area of trend, or leverage or private-management planning. These latter types of planning seem likely to result in effects which favour business interests.

Figure 3.1 A typology of planning styles.

Perceived nature of urban problems	Attitude to market processes	
	Market-critical redressing imbalances and inequalities created by the market	Market-led correcting inefficiencies while supporting market processes
Buoyant area: minor problems and buoyant market	REGULATIVE	TREND
Marginal area: pockets of urban problems and potential market interest	POPULAR	LEVERAGE
Derelict area: comprehensive urban problems and depressed market	PUBLIC INVESTMENT	PRIVATE MANAGEMENT

Source: Brindley et al. (1989: 9).

The main problem with this study is that the authors offer no evidence on the representative nature of the selected case studies. They therefore cannot tell us how often the different styles of planning are found nor whether they constitute an exhaustive list of planning styles.

In summarizing the findings of these types of study Reade says:

That some of them show us how powerful developers can extract concessions from planning authorities, that others show us how apparently powerless residents' and environmentalist protest groups can nevertheless sometimes get what they want, and yet others of them concentrate on demonstrating the bumbling dilatoriness of officialdom, or the ways in which the planners collude with powerful private sector interests (Reade 1987:73).

But he goes on to point out that the choice of case study depends very much on the special interests of the researchers involved. Taken together, all the studies summarized above cannot claim to be a statistically valid sample of the way in which particular interests come to be incorporated as inputs to planning policies. This point must be addressed when seeking to study planning outputs and their effects.

On the other hand, it is also fair to point out how consistently these studies show that developers are often more powerful than local planning authorities; that political interests rather than rationality guide the actions of planners; and that there are often widespread discrepancies between the public objectives of planning and their private outcomes. It is also worth noting that, as with the critiques outlined in Chapter 2, there has been little or no research by planners themselves to rebut these arguments apart from the recent Department of the Environment's planning research programme. There are few professions that could afford to ignore such fundamental criticisms.

Effects

Reade (1987) argues that the analysis of the effects of planning should be divided into two stages. "First, we [sh]ould try to discover the effects which the planning system has had on the pattern of land-use and on the physical form of development . . . [Secondly, we should] go on to investigate the economic and social effects of these 'planned' spatial patterns and built forms" (Reade 1987: 74). This will form the basis of the approach to analyzing the effects of planning in California and Britain in Chapters 5 and 6.

The seminal starting point for such studies in Britain is *The containment of urban England* (1973) by Peter Hall et al. Because this is such an important work it will form the base line from which much analysis of the effects of British planning must start.

In order to overcome the problem of defining a statistically valid sample of case studies, the authors took as their geographic area of study the whole of the main urbanized area of England. This stretches from London in the south east, through Birmingham in the Midlands to Liverpool in the north west. It is variously described as the coffin or hourglass of England. Within this large area the researchers confirmed that there were two main physical consequences and three major socio-economic effects of the British land-use planning system.

The first of the two physical consequences is containment. By this is meant that the quantity of rural land converted to urban uses has been minimized and compacted. This has been achieved by the establishment of Green Belts around the major cities; by concentrating development beyond the Green Belts in limited locations; and by raising residential densities. As a result residential densities in post-war Britain are higher than pre-war densities and those in other countries such as America.

Containment has not, however, prevented decentralization and de-urbanization in Britain. People have continued to leave the big cities in large numbers. But, as with most longer distance migrations, such movement has been economically and socially selective. With the exception of public authority new towns and peripheral estates, those moving out of the cities have been the economically better-off who could afford to buy their own homes.

The second main physical effect of planning has been suburbanization. By this the authors mean the increasing separation of home from work. This leads directly to functionally inefficient commuting, particularly where commuters insist on using their, or more often their companies', cars. This has bred congestion and demands for urban motorways which have been so destructive particularly of working-class housing.

The first economic consequence of these physical effects has, until the 1990s anyway, been rising land and property values. By concentrating all development on to a relatively restricted supply of urban land, the planning system effectively raised its price and forced developers to raise housing densities.

The second economic consequence of planning is that, as predicted by Friedman (1962, 1980), the rate of economic growth has probably been reduced. The imposition of planning controls has inhibited the spread of manufacturing industry into the suburbs and the countryside. The guardians of suburban and rural amenity have prevented this. Thus amenity has been traded off against economic growth.

The third social consequence of planning is the regressive distribution of physical environmental advantages and disadvantages, and also opportunities for the acquisition of wealth and income. The costs of environmental deterioration, increased housing and transport costs and lower rates of capital appreciation of property values have been borne mainly by the urban underprivileged tenants of public housing and tenants in private rented property. The corresponding benefits in physical environments, value for money in housing and faster than average capital appreciation of house values have accrued mainly to middle-class ruralites and the new owner-occupier suburbanites.

Again, as with the theoretical critiques of planning outlined in Chapter 2 and the critical studies of the manipulation of planning policies, there have been no serious attempts by the planning profession to produce evidence that the effects of planning are any different from those described above. This constitutes a remarkably ostrich-like attitude on the part of the profession on the need to justify its very existence in the face of intellectual criticisms and political attacks.

Conclusions

In retrospect, the 1980s may be seen as a time of sea-change in attitudes to and the activities of public planning in general and land-use planning in particular. The combination of economic recession and depression with intellectual and political attacks on planning led to major changes in public planning practice in California, Britain and Yugoslavia. In California Reaganomics combined with voter reluctance to fund public authorities led to major changes in what they could do. In Britain Thatcherism and its acceleration of economic decline resulted in the removal of many activities from public planning to markets and the drastic curtailment of funding for local collective activities. In Yugoslavia, at the end of the decade, public planning collapsed almost completely. These were momentous events which hankering after a return to post-war practices will not change.

The responses by planning theorists and practitioners to intellectual critiques and political changes have been either non-existent or ineffective. It has been argued here that an essential first step in producing such a response must be to identify what effects particular planning policies have brought about in the past. This involves the introduction of both systematic evaluations of past planning and independent monitoring of future policies.

CHAPTER FOUR
Research design and methods

Introduction

In order to develop the knowledge of what planning does by monitoring the effects of its activities we need consistent and systematic methods. This raises special problems in the social sciences and policy areas such as planning. These problems revolve around the question of whether and how far the methods of the natural sciences can be employed or are appropriate in studying an activity such as planning.

The first section of this chapter evaluates the difficulties of using the methods of the natural sciences in the fields of human behaviour, politics and planning. In this section on the logic of such methods it is concluded that they are not appropriate in planning.

The second section advocates the use of the classic method of the social sciences – namely the comparative method. The use of this method is advocated because people cannot be confined to laboratories for experimental purposes. In addition, monitoring the effects of public policies can only take place after they have been implemented for some period of time. This type of research, therefore, has to be both comparative and historical.

The final, third section describes the sources used in the comparative studies carried out in California and Britain. Material is extracted from them according to five major and consistent questions. These are what effects has land-use planning had on:

(a) urban containment?

(b) suburbanization?

(c) land and house prices?

(d) economic growth?

(e) residential and social segregation?

Logic

The research method that the natural sciences are thought to employ is called the "hypothetico-deductive method"" It is illustrated in Figure 4.1.

Figure 4.1 The hypothetico-deductive method.

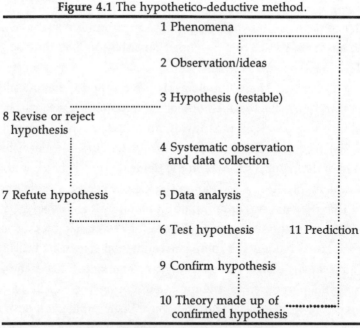

Source: McNeill, P. & C. Townley (1986).

The process starts with phenomena (1). These are parts of the real world. They can be observed objectively (2). Such observations prompt hypotheses (3). These are intelligent and testable guesses about why the phenomena take the form that they do. Tests of such hypotheses can be conducted in laboratories or by collecting more data in the field. The main aim of such tests is **to prove the hypothesis wrong**. It only has to be proved wrong once in order to know that it is incorrect. To do this, experiments are carried out or data collected (4). The results of these exercises are analyzed (5). The hypothesis is then tested against these results (6). If the hypothesis is not supported by the evidence it should be rejected (7), revised (8), and a new hypothesis formulated (3) . If it is supported (9), it can be seen as a contribution to theory. As more pieces of evidence are collected together theories can be used to predict (11) future phenomena.

Reade (1987) advocates a theoretical model based on the hypothetico-deductive method for monitoring planning. He derives this from Karl Popper (1945, 1957). Popper argued that

All government policies, indeed all executive and administrative decisions, involve empirical predictions: if we do X, Y will follow: on the other hand, if we want to achieve B we must do A. . . . A policy is a hypothesis which has to be tested against reality and corrected in the light of experience. . . . *The implementation of every policy needs to be tested, and this is done not by looking for evidence that one's efforts are having the desired effects, but by looking for evidence that they are not* (emphasis added; see Magee 1973: 75–7).

The Popperian approach advocated by Reade (1987) is a looser and less precise social science version of the experimental method used in laboratories by natural scientists. Even so it only has limited applications in social science in general and planning in particular. There are three reasons for this.

First, most human social interactions cannot be abstracted from the real world and manipulated in laboratory-type experiments. Some psychologists such as Milgram (1965), Haney et al. (1973) and Atkinson et al. (1975) have conducted exemplary experiments of this type. But they have been tightly defined and single-issue research. In most cases their conditions could not be replicated in plan monitoring.

Secondly, the Popperian method is, in any case, only appropriate to the analysis of future planning policies and not to past ones. This is because historical variables are now past and cannot be altered in any way in order to conduct experiments with them. Any such attempts can now only be speculation.

Thirdly, the method is more appropriate to the inanimate objects with which natural scientists deal than to intelligent human beings. The problem with the latter is that they can alter their behaviour as a result of new knowledge. This then invalidates previous hypotheses about what it would be without the introduction of new knowledge or changed circumstances.

Nevertheless, the Popperian model has been used in limited experiments variously known as action or evaluative research. The best example of this approach was the Community Development Programmes of the 1970s. In these, researchers were actively involved in planning and introducing changes in local policies. They then monitored the effects of these policies.

The Community Development Programmes gave rise to two main problems which would also bedevil attempts to use the same method to monitor the effects of planning. The first was that they were established on the basis of assumptions, in their case about the individual causes of poverty, which eventually proved to be inadequate. Secondly, when the monitoring results pointed this out, they were soon brought to an end, in the late 1970s, by the policy makers and politicians who did not like these findings.

This illustrates the probability that independent monitoring of the effects of planning would be politically and professionally unpopular. Those involved in public planning and administration are dealing with complex and changing circumstances. All too often the outcomes of their policies will not be what they envisaged. Over time both the circumstances with which they are dealing and their own policies will drift away from their original characteristics and intentions. The credibility of planning is not advanced, however, by simply ignoring these problems, as has often been the case in the past. If planners cannot or will not monitor the effects of planning, this lends weight to the arguments of those who would like to replace public administration by private markets. Without the monitoring of costs and benefits flowing from public administration it can just as easily be asserted that the use of private markets would produce similar or "better" results at less cost.

It is concluded from this discussion that any method for monitoring the effects of past planning policies must be able to overcome two main problems. First, it cannot entail the use of hypothetico-deductive logic because that cannot be applied to past policies and will be highly contentious even if applied in the future. Secondly, the paucity of past studies means that it is difficult to arrive at statistically valid samples based on individual case studies.

The comparative method

The method advocated here to overcome these difficulties is the comparative method. In sociology the comparative method has been considered to be *The Method* in much the same way as the hypothetico-deductive method has been *The Method* in the natural sciences. Its use in sociology dates back to Auguste Comte who employed it to produce "laws" of societal development. Karl Marx also used the method in support of his materialist conception of history. The work of Max Weber and Emile Durkheim, founding fathers of sociology, was based on the use of the comparative method.

More recent sociological research, with particular relevance to planning, has relied almost exclusively on the comparative method. This work is concerned with the sociology of development. Although much of it has focused primarily on the origins and continuation of poverty and its consequences in Third World countries, it also has direct applications in the understanding of British cities as shown by, for example, Mellor (1977).

The comparative method is fundamental to causal explanation in social science and policy analysis. Its basic technique is to make comparisons of instances where the phenomenon to be explained is present and instances where it is absent. In planning, for example, this involves describing and analyzing such phenomena as land-uses in circumstances where planning is present and other circumstances where it is absent. Other things being equal, the differences in land-uses between two such sets of circumstances can then be used to identify and assess the effects of planning on land-uses.

It is argued here that the major effect of British land-use planning has been urban containment. In order to assess the magnitude and characteristics of this effect and its consequences it is therefore necessary to examine instances where it has been absent and compare those with examples where it has been present. The example used here where no containment policies were operating is Californian planning before 1972. This is the year when the first growth management policy was introduced in Petaluma. Even today, most cities in California do not have a policy of urban containment. Thus the effects of urban containment can be analyzed in California by comparing areas where it is not a policy with those in which growth management policies have been introduced.

Even where growth management policies have been introduced they are not as absolute and permanent as their equivalents in Britain. Here containment has generally been enforced more rigorously in southern as compared with northern Britain. The effects of these differences can therefore also be compared with the effects of the absence or varying degrees of containment in California.

The comparisons of the effects of planning made in this book therefore run along a continuum from:

(a) no containment (California before 1972 and today);
(b) growth management (California in cities and counties which have adopted growth management policies);
(c) relaxed containment (in the northeast of England);
(d) tough containment (in the southeast of England).

The use of the comparative method employing examples selected from along this continuum is summarized in Figure 4.2.

California with no growth management will be used as the base line with which to compare subsequent degrees of planning between and within different planning regimes. This base line will be compared, in Chapter 5, with the effects of growth management in California. In Chapter 6, the effects of varying degrees of soft and hard containment in Britain will be examined.

Figure 4.2 The comparative method and monitoring land-use planning.

Planning regimes	Degrees of urban containment			
	None	Low	Medium	High
California	No growth management			
		With growth management		
Britain			Relaxed containment	
				Tough containment

Sources

The sources of information used for making these comparisons will be secondary sources. Apart from the time and cost limitations on collecting primary material, there have been scattered research projects which can now be brought together in order to provide adequate information on the effects of different planning regimes. The starting point for many of these studies is *Containment of urban England* by Hall et al. (1973), particularly Chapter 12 of Volume 2. This provides the intellectual structure for the two following chapters on California and Britain.

Much of the empirical material on the effects of planning in California is provided by research carried out at the University of California, Berkeley. The British equivalent is drawn mainly from research at the University of Reading and the DoE's planning research programme. The detailed sources are given in the text.

Conclusions

Hall et al. (1973) have produced the most comprehensive evaluation of the effects of past British planning policies to date. They showed that the main effects of post-war British planning had been containment, suburbanization, rising land and property values, reduction in the rate of economic growth and the regressive distribution of physical environmental advantages and disadvantages, and also opportunities for the acquisition of wealth and income.

In order to assess the continued validity of these findings and to evaluate the probable effects of future planning policies, the use of the comparative method is advocated. In this study it is argued that situations of minimal planning should be used as the base lines from which to compare increasing degrees of planning intervention and their effects. California is used as the lowest level planning regime in this study. It is not claimed that there is no planning at all in California, any more than it is true to say this of Houston which is often cited as an example of least planning. What is argued is that great importance is attached to the operation of markets and high significance is accorded to individual property rights in California which greatly circumscribes the potential rôles of planning there. It is also the case that before the 1970s there were no policies for urban containment in California. Even since that decade, local growth management policies do not prevent urban expansion completely, as Green Belts do in Britain. The effects of these Californian policies are compared with those of relaxed containment in the north and tough containment in the south of England

Chapters 5 & 6 will describe the main identifiable effects of planning in California and Britain. It must be emphasized, however, that the comparative method is not just concerned with descriptions of similarities and differences in different places. The main point of the comparisons is not just description but explanation.

Before containment and after growth management: California

Introduction

Chapter 5 focuses on the Californian land-use planning system and its effects. The chapter is divided into five main sections. These are:

(a) containment;

(b) suburbanization;

(c) land and housing prices;

(d) economic growth;

(e) residential and social segregation.

The first section examines the containment – or lack of containment – of Californian cities. It is shown not to have been a major objective of Californian planning. The result has been the growth of cities like Los Angeles. Growth management movements are a comparatively recent phenomenon in California.

The second section describes the effects of suburbanization. These have been based on the rapid spread of car ownership and a huge freeway building programme. Suburbanization is shown to be a complex phenomenon because, on the one hand, the lack of containment policies has allowed many jobs and workers to move to the suburbs, but, on the other hand, housing scarcity and rising costs have still forced workers to commute up to 70 miles both to and from work.

The third section examines the relationships between land and house prices. Both are shown to be increased in various ways after the introduction of growth management policies and the consequent containment of some cities.

The fourth section looks at the relationships between economic growth and the costs of planning. These are shown to add to the cost of housing through delays and extra interest charges. These are the direct costs of planning imposed on developers and then usually passed on to property purchasers. On the other hand, inflation is shown to be more important than planning in adding extra costs to housing.

The fifth section analyzes the main social effect of land-use planning. This is the increase in residential and, therefore, social segregation. This has resulted partly from the funding arrangements for private housing and partly from exclusionary zoning practices. It has not been counterbalanced by any major public housing programmes.

Containment

Introduction

Containment is defined here as the process by which the quantity of rural land converted to urban uses is minimized and compacted. In Britain it has been achieved by the establishment of Green Belts around the major cities; by concentrating development beyond the Green Belts in limited locations; and by raising residential densities. As a result residential densities in post-war Britain are higher than pre-war densities and those in other countries such as America (Hall et al. 1973).

In the Californian planning system the balance of its guiding principles is characterized by the dominance of the interests of individual private property owners operating in modified market conditions. The result of this dominance have been that there are no state-wide policies

44

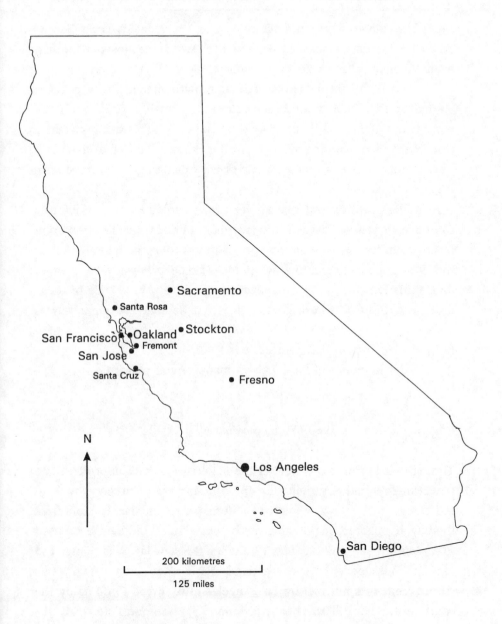

Figure 5.1 California: major cities and towns.

for urban containment in California. The Los Angeles–Long Beach–
Anaheim Standard Consolidated Statistical Area is the most outstanding
example of the absence of such a policy (Fig. 5.1).

Even with the introduction of local growth management policies,
started by Petaluma in 1972, absolute and permanent urban containment is not a planning policy found in California. This distinguishes it
from the British planning system. For this reason, the Californian planning system is used as the example of least planning to compare with
Britain.

Attitudes towards and policies for urban containment in California
can nevertheless be divided into two main periods. In the first period
lasting until the 1970s, there was little support for containment. During
the 1970s support began to grow and was first expressed in the form of
local initiatives for growth management policies. The effects of these
different attitudes towards containment will be analyzed separately as
follows:

(a) pre-1970s no containment policies;
(b) the development of local growth management policies.

Pre-1970s no containment policies

Throughout both periods neither the Federal nor the Californian State
Governments had any policy for the containment of urban growth in
the United States as a whole or California in particular. In California
there were no effective planning mechanisms that could have been used
to contain urban growth before 1971 when the state law was changed to
require consistency between general plans and zoning. Even this
requirement was not met by Los Angeles until forced to do so by the
courts in the late 1980s. Thus, as Marion Clawson and Peter Hall cor-
rectly observed,

In spite of many similarities of geography, economics, and government, Britain and the United States have greatly different –
even fully opposite – attitudes toward the form of desirable urban
growth. While the United States has permitted and even encouraged low-density, discontiguous urban growth that leap-frogs

into the countryside around the cities, Britain since World War II has operated a quite strict and notably successful policy of urban containment. The contrast is particularly striking, because in many other respects both countries have experienced similar social and economic trends, and both have shared some common policies; thus both have had rising populations and more households, rising affluence, and higher car ownership, and both have in effect encouraged mass owner occupancy of single-family homes. Many of the forces working for rapid urban spread, in other words, have been present in both countries; but in Britain they have been countered by a strong and effective system of physical planning, which has not been present in the United States (Clawson & Hall 1973: 5–6).

Despite having no policy of urban containment, Table 5.1 shows that only some 4 per cent of the 48 contiguous states of the USA had been urbanized by the end of the 1970s. This included urbanized areas and urban places (2%), rural roads, railroads and airports (1%) and military and nuclear installations (1%). Such figures would make it difficult to argue for a policy of containment on the grounds of land scarcity.

Table 5.1 Major uses of land in the contiguous United States.

	Per cent of 48 states' area
Rural uses	
Forests outside parks	32
Grassland pasture and range	31
Cropland	24
Wetlands, bare rock, desert and tundra	5
Rural parks and wildlife reserves	3
Farmsteads on farms	1
Urban uses	
Urbanized areas and urban places	2
Rural roads, railroads and airports	1
Military and nuclear installations	1
TOTAL ACRES = 100%	1,897.9 million

Source: Frey (1979: 27–33)

During the second period, starting in the 1970s and accelerating during the 1980s, however, there have been growing efforts to contain urban growth. Often growth controls are the product of citizen-sponsored initiatives. Citizens' groups have also managed to curtail growth through litigation based upon environmental protection statutes, such as the California Environmental Quality Act. Local residents have also managed to stop or reduce development through political opposition (Frieden 1979). The State of California has stood aloof from these movements so far. But other states, notably Florida and New Jersey, have developed concerns about traffic congestion and urban sprawl since the mid-1980s. These movements are comparatively recent, however, and it is necessary to describe and explain the growth of Californian cities without their intervention until well into the 1970s.

During the post Second World War period economic, population and household growth led to the rapid contiguous expansion of most of California's major cities. This expansion involved decentralization from the original central cities and the large-scale expansion of their surrounding suburban rings. Table 5.2 shows continuing large-scale population growth during the 1970s in places such as Orange County, San Diego and San Jose. It also shows that by the 1980s between 51 and 77 per cent of the residents of some of California's major cities lived outside the central cities and in their suburbs.

Table 5.2 Population changes in major Californian cities 1970–80. Total Standard Metropolitan Statistical Areas (SMSAs) and suburban populations.

SMSA	Population change 1970–80 (%)	Proportion living outside central city 1980 (%)
Los Angeles	6	54
Orange County	36	77
San Diego	37	51
San Jose	22	57
San Francisco	5	66

Source: US Department of Commerce, Bureau of the Census (1973, 1983). *Census of population: general population characteristics, United States summary,* Washington, US Government Printing Office.

The two most important institutions that facilitated the suburbanization of American and Californian cities were the Federal Housing

Administration (FHA) and large-scale private builders. The FHA provided loans and the builders constructed mass-produced housing.

The FHA was established in 1934 when the Congress enacted the National Housing Act. According to Jackson (1985: 205), "No agency of the United States government has had a more pervasive and powerful impact on the American people over the past half-century than the FHA". Although the programme was designed to improve housing standards, to create dependable financing with reasonable terms and to stabilize a faltering mortgage market, it was primarily an employment programme aimed at reinvigorating the extremely important building industry.

In 1944, FHA was joined by the Servicemen's Readjustment Act, which helped returning servicemen buy housing. It was popularly known as the GI Bill. Both of these programmes were designed to insure long-term mortgage loans made by lenders for home construction and sale.

According to Jackson, FHA and the GI Bill revolutionized the housing finance industry in the following four ways:

(a) Before the introduction of these programmes, mortgages were normally limited two-thirds to one-half of the appraised value. These programmes allowed buyers access to housing with down payments of 10 per cent or less.

(b) Mortgages were 25 to 30 years and fully amortized. This lowered monthly payments and the rate of default.

(c) FHA established minimum standard building construction, which have become essentially an industry standard.

(d) By insuring mortgages, the government reduced the risk to lenders, which in turn allowed interest rates to decrease by two or three percentage points (Jackson 1985: 204).

As a result of these changes, the number of Americans that could potentially buy a home expanded dramatically. Relatively few government programs could match the FHA's record of success:

Housing starts rose to 332,000 in 1937, to 399,000 in 1938, to 458,000 in 1939, to 530,000 in 1940, and to 619,000 in 1941. This was a startling lift from the 93,000 starts of 1933. After World War II, the numbers became even larger, and by the end of 1972, FHA had helped nearly eleven million families to own houses and

another twenty-two million families to improve their properties.
. . . Between 1934 and 1972, the percentage of American families living in owner-occupied dwellings rose from 44 per cent to 63 per cent (Jackson 1985: 205).

Thanks to FHA and GI Bill financing, it was often cheaper to buy a home in the suburbs than to rent in the city (Clawson & Hall 1973: 16–17; Jackson 1985: 205–6). For example,

In the early 1950s families living in the Kew Gardens section of Queens were paying about ninety dollars per month for small two-bedroom apartments. For less money, they could, and often did, move to the new Levittown-type developments springing up along the highways from Manhattan. Even the working classes could aspire to home ownership. . . . Not surprisingly, the middle-class suburban family with the new house and the long-term, fixed-rate, FHA-insured mortgage became a symbol, and perhaps a stereotype, of the American way of life (Jackson 1985: 206).

From 1948 to 1968, the average annual increase in the consumer price index was slightly over 2 per cent. Thus, home owners also had a hedge against inflation that was not available to renters (Clawson & Hall 1973: 17).

The second important factor in the growth of American suburbs was the large scale private builder. The large builder had the capacity "to take raw suburban land, divide it into parcels and streets, install needed services, apply mass production methods to residential construction, and sell the finished product to unprecedented numbers of consumers" (Checkoway 1984: 153). The rise of large builders was a national trend. In 1938, 5 per cent of all the new houses in the nation were built by large builders; by 1959, they built 64 percent (Checkoway 1984: 155).

The large builders were the Henry Ford of housing. They bought supplies in bulk directly from the producer, maintained high inventories, developed sophisticated subcontracting methods, created a specialized labour force, used prefabricated materials and developed other mass-production building techniques (Checkoway 1984: 156). Like Ford, they produced a more modest and repetitive product at a much lower price. The classic example is Levittown on Long Island, New York.

In 1947 Levitt acquired 14,000 acres of Long Island farmland about 30 miles from New York City and proceeded to revolutionize the house-building industry. By 1948 Levitt was completing more than 35 houses per day and 150 houses per week and rapidly selling the low-cost product. More than 17,000 identical houses for over 70,000 people were finally built side-by-side in uniform rows and sold for the same price of $7990. By 1950 "Levittown" was praised as "an accomplishment of heroic proportions" and the Levitt house was known as "the best house for the money in the United States" (Checkoway 1984: 157).

Despite their repetitiousness, the houses sold rapidly and the trend for the future was set.

In contrast, the small builder, who had formerly dominated the market, was not capable of producing houses in the quantities needed to overcome the shortages. He "could not employ a permanent labour force, develop a research staff, bargain for materials in volume at lower cost, or buy a substantial area of land for large-scale development" (Checkoway 1984: 154).

The growing dominance of the large builder in the San Francisco Bay Area was documented by Maisel (1953) and Herzog (1963). In 1949, large and medium builders comprised only 2 per cent of the local total but accounted for 55 per cent of the houses produced. Follow-up studies showed that between 1950 and 1960 large builders increased their share to 74 per cent of all houses produced. By 1960 large builders built three out of every four houses in this area (Checkoway 1984, citing Maisel 1953; Herzog 1963: 19–32).

Large builders needed large expanses of cheap land. Such land was often unavailable within the cities or too expensive to clear (Clawson & Hall 1973: 15–16; Checkoway 1984: 156). As a result, large builders went to the suburbs or "leap-frogged""to the virgin countryside to build their subdivisions. Builders were able to create this discontiguous type of development for the following reasons:

(a) Before 1971, towns, cities and counties did not have legally binding general plans that could have restricted growth to land contiguous with existing urbanized areas.

(b) The car freed Americans from reliance on public transportation.

(c) Septic systems and wells freed developments from public services – at least until these private systems failed (Clawson & Hall 1973).

(d) Even if the lots were too small for septic systems, most jurisdictions utilized the postage stamp fee system for the extension of new sewage lines. Under this system, a developer was charged the same hook-up fee whether the new development was contiguous with existing development or several miles from the closest sewer line.

(e) Through local taxes, this inefficiency was borne by existing residents, so they subsidized new growth.

(f) Similarly, the cost of new schools and parks was not borne by the new subdivision, but by all tax-payers.

The main effect of uncontained urban growth during the post Second World War years was to provide millions of American families with relatively inexpensive single-family houses on quarter-acre plots of land. For those who could afford to leave the central cities or wanted to form new households this was a very desirable outcome, and one that could not have been accomplished had there been a nationwide policy of urban containment. It led to the large-scale growth of suburban housing as shown in Table 5.2. But even with this large-scale transfer of rural to urban land-uses only 4 per cent of the 48 contiguous states were urbanized by the end of the 1970s, as shown in Table 5.1.

The development of local growth management policies

Despite this, two phenomena led to the period of pro-containment in California. The first was high rates of growth. The second was the passage of Proposition 13, in 1978, which reduced dramatically property taxes throughout the state. Suddenly many local governments found themselves facing a burgeoning population and a shrinking tax base.

Growth in the San Francisco Bay Area, for example, has been very rapid. Between 1950 and 1960 the Bay Area grew by 1 million persons. It repeated this feat between 1960 and 1970 (Dowall 1984). It grew by almost a further 900,000 persons between 1980 and 1990 (1990 US Census). In some cities, this growth strained water and sewer systems; in others it led to overcrowded schools and traffic congestion.

52

Cities that were already having trouble keeping pace with growth received another blow when the statewide initiative Proposition 13 passed in 1978. All through the 1960s and 1970s Californians saw housing prices increase. In the 1970s prices were sky-rocketing. As a consequence, property taxes were going through the ceiling. In some cases, long-time home owners were paying more in property taxes than in house payments. This led to the passage of Proposition 13, which required property valuations to be rolled back to 1975–6 levels and set a ceiling of 1 per cent on all future property taxes.

The result of Proposition 13 was that new residential development could not pay its way through property taxes alone. It caused some local governments to alter their attitudes toward residential development. First, some communities began to compete for commercial development at the expense of residential development. Commercial development would produce sales tax revenue and higher property tax revenue without adding any extra burden to such services as schools, parks and libraries. Secondly, virtually all local governments began to impose an increasing array of development fees and impact fees. Thirdly, more communities enacted stringent growth management policies (GMPs).

There is no doubt that GMPs are increasingly common. In 1972 the American Society of Planning Officials identified about one dozen communities nationwide with growth controls. In 1974 a new study showed that over 200 communities were actively attempting to control growth (Dowall 1984: 3). In 1975, in the Bay Area, over one half of all communities actively attempted to limit growth in some manner (Dowall 1984: 4). A statewide survey conducted by the California State Office of Planning and Research (OPR) found that over 300 of the 445 local planning agencies in the state were attempting to control the rate of land-use development through either growth management or more traditional techniques of land-use management (Dowall 1984: 30). The latest study by Glickfeld & Levine (1992) shows that by 1988 California's counties and cities had passed a total of 907 growth control measures.

Two illustrative examples of GMPs are San Jose and Fresno. In 1976, San Jose established an Urban Services Boundary, a line beyond which essential public infrastructure would not be extended. The boundary was not intended to restrict the number of new homes, but instead to slow the rate of rural land conversion by promoting higher residential densities and encouraging infill development (Landis 1986: 11).

The city of Fresno established a different system in 1977 called the Fresno Urban Growth Management System (UGM system). Fresno County and the city of Fresno had already developed a "county referral plan", which usually required the developers of unincorporated land to have their property annexed to the cities of Fresno or Clovis before permits would be issued. Moreover, development would be directed towards infill and urban fringe areas. The UGM system further required all developers to pay the full costs of extending essential city services.

In 1980, builders of single-family detached homes in urban fringe areas paid as much as $5,000 per unit, while projects in built up areas typically paid less than $2,000 per unit (Landis 1986: 12). Thus, the system was intended to charge for the true cost of development and thereby to encourage a tighter pattern of development.

Attempts to contain urban growth in California by the use of GMPs are relatively new. Monitoring studies of their effects have concentrated so far mainly on their impacts on land values and house prices. The results of these studies will be summarized in a separate section on that topic below.

At the moment there is not much hard information on whether they have achieved any of their stated goals. These are usually a combination of:

(a) requiring development to pay its own way;
(b) easing school overcrowding;
(c) reducing traffic congestion;
(d) reducing air and water pollution;
(e) alleviating water shortages;
(f) preserving open space;
(g) preserving the local quality of life.

None of these corresponds to the main aim of British containment, which was to stop urban sprawl.

While some studies have attempted to measure community satisfaction with growth control, Deakin (1989: 12–13) points out that they lack hard evidence and are ambiguous. As for traffic congestion, growth control probably takes too narrow a view, because trip-making for existing residents is increasing and more trips into many cities are non-local (Deakin 1989: 13–14). Growth control fails to address these issues.

Although GMPs are controversial, Deakin (1989) asserts that

Majority support for these policies has been found here in California and elsewhere among low-income people, among minorities, among blue-collar workers, and among the elderly, as well as among professional classes. In fact, the group that seems to least support growth control consists of young, educated, wealthy, professionals who work in real estate and private enterprise (Deakin 1990: 5).

It should be noted, however, that this support comes from those who already live in the community and not from those who wish to move there. Deakin also asserts that the studies that attempt to link growth control to educated, white, higher-income groups are weak or inconclusive (Deakin 1989: 7–8).

What does seem to emerge from this review is that growth controls are supported politically and used by existing residents to reduce the numbers of new houses built in their areas. This has the effect of restraining new demands for urban services and reducing the flow of newcomers to their localities.

Suburbanization

Introduction

Suburbanization is defined here as the increasing separation of home and work. This may lead to functionally inefficient commuting particularly where commuters insist on using their, or more often their companies', cars. In Britain, this has bred congestion and demands for urban motorways which have been so destructive particularly of working-class housing (Hall et al. 1973).

The relationships between home and work in America have changed through time. After the Second World War the mass movement to the suburbs increased the separation between centrally located jobs and the new suburban housing. Market adjustments were made to these changing circumstances by employers. They began moving employment to the suburbs. This market-led movement of employment to suburban locations decreased the potential separation between home and work.

Since the 1970s, however, the combination of continued market-led suburban job growth combined with public intervention in the supply of housing, as a result of growth management policies and Proposition 13, have increased the separation between work and home. It is possible to compare the pre-GMP and Proposition 13 era with the 1980s in order to assess the effects of these planning and plan-related public policies on the separation of homes and work.

Suburbanization will be analyzed in terms of:

(a) the journey to work;
(b) population and employment decentralization;
(c) growing separation between home and work.

The journey to work

The post- Second World War movement to the growing suburbs was made possible in America not by the use of public rail transport but by the development of the mass-produced motor car and the national freeway system. President Eisenhower was convinced that both were necessary for national defence and to create an economic boom. As a result, he threw his support behind the construction of a national freeway system, which led to the 1956 Federal-Aid Highway Act. This introduced a system of taxes on petrol, oil, buses and trucks which raised some $41 billion and led to the construction of 41,000 miles of new roads (Hall 1988: 291–2).

The results of the development of this extensive new freeway system on the separation of work and home are indicated in Table 5.3. This shows that, by the end of the 1970s, the traditional journey to work from the suburbs to central cities represented only one fifth of all journeys to work. In contrast, suburb to suburb commuting represented twice as many journeys at two fifths of the total.

Table 5.3 Trends in origin–destination mixes of work trips within all US urbanized areas, 1975 and 1980.

Commute pattern	1975	1980
Central city to central city	33	33
Suburb to central city	20	20
Suburb to suburb	39	40
Central city to suburb (reverse commute)	8	7
TOTAL N = 100%	49,421,000	63,125,000

Sources: US Department of Commerce, Bureau of the Census (1979, 1984), 1980 Census of population. *Journey to work – metropolitan commuting flows.* Washington: Government Printing Office. Department of Commerce, Bureau of the Census (1979), *Journey to work in the United States: 1975.* Washington: Government Printing Office.

Population and employment decentralization

Table 5.2 reflects the fact that the American people had been filling up the suburbs. Between 1950 and 1980, the suburban population "nearly tripled, from 35.2 million to 101.5 million – representing about 45 per cent of the nation's total population. During the same period, central cities grew only modestly, from 50 million to 68 million" (Cervero 1986: 3–4).

The movement of white-collar and bloused workers to the suburbs coincided with changes in the occupational structure of the American economy. "Nationally, the share of jobs in manufacturing has fallen from 32 per cent right after the Second World War to 24 per cent in the early 1980s. The service sector, including jobs in office, retail, government, education, and entertainment, grew from 49 per cent to 66 per cent of total employment during this same period" (Cervero 1986: 8). This "white-collarization" of employment freed companies from the necessity to locate near the rail spurs and ports of the big cities.

Once free from the old locational constraints of central cities, firms could take advantage of the growing suburbs and freeway network. The advantages of then moving to the suburbs have been summarized by Cervero (1985). He argues that

Among high-tech firms, the existence of high-skilled labour usually tops the list. To help recruit and maintain engineers and professional staff, many firms have been attracted to the aesthetics and roominess of a campus office park setting. Moreover, the steady flight of families to the suburbs throughout the 1960s and 1970s has created vast pools of workers, particularly married women. . . .

Concerns over rising inner-city crime rates, congestion, and the lack of affordable housing for workers have also influenced corporate relocation decisions. The generally lower cost-of-living levels in suburban areas, moreover, have meant potential salary savings to businesses who locate there.

Sky-rocketing land and rental costs in many downtown areas have likewise prompted corporations to relocate their mid-management and back office staffs to outlying locations. . . . The rapid acceleration of telecommunications technologies has enabled many businesses to spin off portions of their operations . . . to less expensive suburban environs.

Furthermore, some suburban communities have successfully lured office investors from central cities by offering incentives. . . . New office developments invariably fatten public treasuries so not surprisingly the competition for these projects is usually spirited (Cervero 1986: 9).

The extent of such employment movement to the suburbs in some of California's major cities may be seen in Tables 5.2 and 5.3. Table 5.4 illustrates how employment growth during the 1970s varied between 23 per cent in Los Angeles up to 79 per cent in nearby Orange County. This compared with an average of 26 per cent for America as a whole. By 1980, a majority, varying from 53 per cent in San Diego and San Jose to 72 per cent in Orange County, of total employment was located outside the central cities. This compared with an average of 48 per cent for America as a whole. With the notable exception of San Jose, the proportion of employment located outside the central cities had been growing during the 1970s.

Table 5.5. shows the growth of white-collar and bloused office-related employment outside some of California's major central cities. Again, with the notable exception of San Jose, this type of employment grew by more in the suburbs during the 1970s than it did in the central cities.

Across the whole of America this difference varied between 15 per cent in central cities up to 116 per cent in the suburbs.

Table 5.4 Employment totals and concentrations outside central cities, California 1970–80.

Standard Metropolitan Statistical Area	Employment growth	Employment outside the city	Change outside central city
Los Angeles	23	55	1
Orange County	79	72	4
San Diego	76	53	5
San Francisco	26	70	6
San Jose	62	53	−7
US AVERAGE	26	48	12

Sources: US Department of Commerce, Bureau of the Census (1973, 1983), *Census of population: social and economic characteristics.*

Table 5.5 Changes in office-related employment in and outside central cities, California 1970–80.

Standard Metropolitan Statistical Area	Change in office related employment	
	Inside central cities	Outside central cities
Los Angeles	21	25
Orange County	56	91
San Diego	58	96
San Francisco	6	37
San Jose	91	43
US average	15	116

Sources: US Department of Commerce, Bureau of the Census (1973, 1983), *Census of population: social and economic characteristics.* Washington: US Government Printing Office.

The overall position is again summarized by Cervero (1985):

Over 80 per cent of all office floorspace in America's suburbs has been built since 1970. By comparison, only 36 per cent of all downtown office buildings have gone up over the past 15 years. Nationwide, the share of total office space outside central cities jumped from 25 per cent in 1970 to 57 per cent in 1984" (Cervero 1986: 1).

The suburbanization of population and employment does not necessarily lead to an increasing separation between home and work. At one stage the reverse was the case as office employment moved to be closer to its workforce. The absence of urban containment policies facilitated this improvement. Deliberate cumulative and mixed zoning policies could have built on these changes and shortened traditional journeys to work in central cities.

Growing separation between home and work

Subsequently, several factors have combined to increase rather than decrease the separation between home and work. These factors are:

(a) continued suburban employment expansion;
(b) inadequate planning and zoning provision for new and affordable housing;
(c) growth management policies.

Dowall (1984) addresses these first two problems using the example of Santa Clara County, the location of the more popularly known "Silicon Valley". He argues that bottle-necks occur when the demand for land and housing exceeds current supply. If a city fails to zone enough land for residential development to meet the demand, existing units will increase in price and demand pressures will spill over into other communities (Dowall 1984: 136).

A shortage of developable land can occur when there is an imbalance between land zoned for employment (commercial, industrial, etc.) and land zoned for housing. Table 5.6 shows how this type of imbalance occurs in Santa Clara County, California. It shows that the overall ratio of zoned jobs to housing is 3:1. This indicates the probability that there will be more jobs than housing for workers in Santa Clara County.

There is already a shortage of affordable housing in Santa Clara County. This is forcing workers to look for cheaper housing in southern Alameda County (Dowall 1984: 136). By forcing residents to look for housing far from work, Santa Clara County is creating a job–housing imbalance that increases the separation between home and work, commute distances and adds to the reduction in air quality. More recently, workers in the Santa Clara Valley have begun to seek housing in the distant Central Valley.

Table 5.6 Jobs versus housing potential in Santa Clara County.

	Job expansion based on local zoning	Housing unit expansion based on local zoning
Palo Alto	3,000	1,300
Mountain View	18,620	3,600
Sunnyvale	12,350	1,680
Santa Clara	23,940	2,826
Cupertino	5,120	4,890
Los Altos	0	238
Los Altos Hills	0	322
Milpitas	29,700	3,648
San Jose	123,475	45,786
Campbell	500	200
Los Gatos	350	395
Saratoga	270	2,271
Monte Serino	0	35
Morgan Hill	21,700	6,475
Gilroy	700	4,875
TOTAL	246,025	78,541

Source: Santa Clara County Manufacturing Group 1980. *Vacant land in Santa Clara County: implications for job growth and housing in the 1980s,* February.
Notes: Overall ratio of jobs to housing = 3:1.

Growth management policies are also having similar effects, although in different ways from containment policies in Britain. In California, growth controls often cause more total land to be converted to residential uses because cities often use large lots as a growth control measure. Larger lots and growth controls also aggravate the separation of jobs and housing because potential new residents are forced by scarcity and price to seek housing in more distant cities. As a result travel times increase and more pollutants are emitted Niebanck (1989).

The net results of these factors is that as offices and people have gone to the suburbs, commuting patterns have changed and lengthened. The traditional commuting pattern, which resembled a spoked wheel with the central city as the hub, has become increasingly chaotic as people commute from suburb to suburb. This has contributed to the fact that the average journey to work in America grew, between 1975 and 1980, from 11.1 miles to 12.1 miles.

61

A further consequence of suburbanization is that some groups have no means of travelling from home to work at all. Because traditional public transport does not work well in highly dispersed suburbs, those who are dependent on such transport have been hurt by suburbanization:

Suburbia's increasing popularity as an employment and commercial site has also heightened inequities in Americans' abilities to access different economic, social, and cultural opportunities. For the nation's transportation underclass (e.g., those without a car, the physically disabled), the scattering of workplaces, shopping malls, and recreational centers along the suburban fringes has physically isolated them more than ever, denying them the chance to fully enter into society's mainstream and take advantage of its offerings. Given the dearth of convenient public transit connections in most suburbs, the nation's window of opportunity is being slammed shut on those who cannot drive a car because they are too poor, too young, or too infirm (Cervero 1986: 219).

The move of offices and industries to the suburbs potentially aggravates the high rates of unemployment of inner-city minorities. Most areas do not have public transportation that could transport inner-city workers to the jobs in the suburbs:

Quite often, there are no reverse-direction or cross-town transit runs connecting core neighbourhoods with outlying business parks and office centres during peak periods. In some cases, the only connection between minority neighbourhoods and outlying areas is an occasional domestic workers shuttle carrying housekeepers and gardeners to fairly affluent suburban neighbourhoods (Cervero 1986: 220).

The emergence of worker shuttles that deliver minorities to the white suburbs for a day of work hints disturbingly of apartheid. There are also accounts of how suburbs have resisted the delivery of public transportation to their communities because they wanted to keep minorities out (Cervero 1986: 220).

Land and housing prices

Introduction

This section addresses the question of the economic repercussions of the physical effects of land-use planning. It looks in particular at the economic effects of the physical containment of urban growth. In Britain this has resulted, until the 1990s anyway, in rising land and property values. By concentrating all development on to a relatively restricted supply of urban land, the planning system effectively raised its price and forced developers to raise housing prices and densities (Hall et al. 1973).

In California, where containment was not a general or common policy before the 1970s, land and housing prices remained low by British standards. After the 1970s when growth management policies were introduced and proliferated several studies have described higher increases in land and property prices in areas with GMPs than in those without them (Dowall 1984, Landis 1986, Zorn et al. 1986, Niebanck 1989). It is clear, therefore, that changes take place in local housing markets, after the introduction of GMPs, that drive up land and property prices. The questions addressed in this section are not only what are the magnitudes of these changes but also why do they take place? They are analyzed under the following two headings:

(a) Growth management policies and increases in land and house prices;

(b) Local oligopolies and increases in land and housing prices.

Growth management policies and increases in land and housing prices

The descriptive question will be addressed first. In order to discover whether there is a correlation between GMPs and additional increases in land and house prices most authors have used the comparative method. They have compared towns that are similar except for the fact that one has a system of growth control.

In *The suburban squeeze*, for example, Dowall (1984) looked at three sets of cities in the San Francisco Bay Area. These were Fremont and Concord; San Rafael and Novato; and Santa Rosa and Napa. The Bay Area is particularly suited for a study of growth control because it has experienced phenomenal growth during the 1960s and 1970s and this led to the widespread adoption of a wide array of growth control measures.

Dowall (1984) argued that local governments can affect the price of land in two ways:

(a) they can restrict the supply of land;

(b) they can reduce the development potential of land.

Governments reduce supply through purchase or condemnation; through moratoriums on annexations and service hook-ups; or through the establishment of urban growth or service boundaries. Governments can decrease the development potential of a particular parcel through down zoning or large lot general plan designations (Dowall 1984: 115). All of the cities which Dowall studied reduced development through one or more of these methods. Although land prices increased in each city, the rate of increase varied.

Dowall (1984) identifies four ways that government land-use regulations can increase housing costs:

(a) they can increase the cost of raw and improved land;

(b) subdivision regulations can require more costly improvements;

(c) approval times can be lengthened thereby increasing financing costs and other overhead expenditures;

(d) the local government can increase hook-up and impact fees (Dowall 1984: 115).

Among these different ways that GMPs increase housing costs, the most important is land costs (Dowall 1984: 111).

Dowall (1984) uses a measure that he calls the "residual value" in his attempt to quantify the inflationary impacts of land-use regulations in the three pairs of communities. The residual value is calculated by subtracting the cost of constructing new units, the costs of land preparation and all required fees and charges from the average house price. The residual value therefore accounts for land and land-holding costs, marketing costs and excess profit. Any difference in residual value between the pairs of cities indicates that housing prices were driven up by land scarcity, monopoly power, or other indirect effects.

Table 5.7. shows that the increase in residual values has varied widely between the cities. But the residual value is always higher in the city in each matched pair which has a GMP.

Table 5.7 Residual values for six San Francisco Bay Area cities 1979 (US$).

| Cities | PRICES | − COSTS | | = RESIDUAL |
	Average house price	Construction cost	Lot improve-ment cost	Fees and charges	Residual value
Concord	92,000	67,310	9,959	2,850	11,881
Fremont	113,800	70,932	10,247	4,350	28,271
Novato	160,700	81,696	13,565	2,200	63,239
San-Rafael	174,200	64,446	17,030	2,855	89,869
Napa	97,800	67,965	17,149	2,665	10,021
Santa-Rosa	90,500	55,442	11,014	2,300	21,744

Source: Dowall (1984).

Dowall (1984) found that the residual values in Fremont continuously increased; the residual value in Concord, its comparison city, increased and then declined. Two reasons for these differing outcomes were, first, that in Concord developers could move their operations to the nearby communities of Pittsburgh and Antioch where land was cheap and plentiful. As a result developers had no incentive to bid up Concord's land prices. Fremont builders had no such outlet. Secondly, Fremont was on the receiving end of the spill-overs from Santa Clara County, where land-use regulations had created a jobs–housing imbalance (Dowall 1984: 169). This point was also demonstrated in the section on suburbanization above.

Although the cities of Napa and Santa Rosa both have Urban Growth Boundaries, the increase in the residual value has been almost twice as high in Santa Rosa. The implementation and enforcement of Santa Rosa's boundary caused developers to bid up prices for large tracts. Santa Rosa is seen by builders as the Bay Area's last frontier. Builders are warehousing land for the future (Dowall 1984: 155–6). By contrast,

Napa is not a big builders market, and large tracts do not need to be warehoused. Moreover, the demand for housing in Napa was much lower, and this lower demand moderates the impacts of a restrictive programme of land-use controls (Dowall 1984: 169).

While the residual values in both San Rafael and Novato have increased dramatically, the timing of the increases shows how development pressures and inflationary land costs can be shifted by land-use policies that restrict development. Marin County has enacted very restrictive growth controls. Growth was first pushed north to San Rafael when the southern Marin cities, which are closer to San Francisco, were built out. Thus, residual values rose rapidly until 1978. At that time, San Rafael itself was largely built out. Although Novato also experienced growth pressures, the residual value sky-rocketed as land zoned for residential purposes in San Rafael diminished and development once again moved north (Dowall 1984: 170).

Zorn et al. (1986) looked at Davis, California, to see if the price and exclusionary impacts of GMPs could be managed better. They begin by pointing out that certain aspects of elasticity in housing demand have not been adequately considered.

First, if effective substitutes for housing in the growth-control community are available (e.g. housing in the neighbouring community), then demand should be more elastic (Zorn et al. 1986: 47). This transfer of demand, however, could have inflationary impacts in the neighbouring community, provided that the supply of housing in the neighbouring community is not adequately elastic (Zorn et al. 1986: 48). Secondly, the demand may be less elastic if the growth-control community has unique amenities. A GMP might actually increase this inelasticity, if the GMP is perceived as protecting or improving these amenities (Zorn et al. 1986: 47).

Zorn et al. describe their analysis as follows:

Specifically, we make the following assumptions:

1 Growth controls significantly restrict supply.

2 Households perceive growth controls as improving community amenities.

3 Old and new housing are not perfect substitutes.

4 Housing in the neighbouring communities is not a perfect

substitute for housing in the growth-controlled community.

Under these circumstances we expect the introduction of growth controls without price-mitigating measures to:

1 Increase the per-unit price of new housing services relative to old housing services in the growth-controlled community.

2 Increase the price of both new and old housing services in the growth-controlled community relative to housing in neighbouring communities.

3 Increase the price of housing services in neighbouring communities (Zorn et al. 1986: 48).

Because Zorn and colleagues want to look at the exclusionary aspects of GMPs, they use the typical and obvious test. This is that if there is a significant reduction in the number of houses that low-income to moderate-income households can buy in the community, the GMP is exclusionary.

Davis is a small university town (pop. 36,640 in 1980), located near Sacramento, California. In 1973 the Davis City Council adopted a GMP that established a population limit of 50,000 by the year 1990. In order to achieve this limit, the GMP would have to lower substantially the rate of growth. The Davis GMP was based upon a building permit allocation system very similar to those of Petaluma and Boulder.

Between April 1975 and May 1982, the city received requests for permits to build 4,667 units, of which only 2,391 were granted (Zorn et al. 1986: 49). Like Petaluma and Boulder, the Davis GMP provided points for low- and moderate-priced housing. Davis, however, went further to encourage the construction of low- and moderate- priced housing. In 1977 Davis implemented a programme which required one third of all units built to be sold at a designated price, which in 1982 was $60,000. After add-ons and corrections for inflation, 25 per cent of these units actually sold for more than $80,000 in 1982 (Zorn et al. 1986: 49). This was still relatively inexpensive by British standards for similar housing.

Davis also passed the Owner-Occupancy Ordinance in 1977, which required the purchasers of all single-family homes to live in the home for 12 months before selling or renting the house. In this way, the city hoped to halt multiple purchases by investors.

Zorn and colleagues compared Davis to the cities of Woodland and

Rancho Cordova, which are approximately the same distance from Sacramento as Davis. They also looked at "actual housing" and "constant quality" housing; the latter was a measure that controlled for variations in quality by predicting prices using a standard quality house for all communities during the entire life of the study (Zorn et al. 1986: 53-4).

Zorn et al. found that after the introduction of the GMP, new houses cost 27 per cent more in Davis and 28 per cent more in the other communities. Thus, new home prices increased by 1 per cent less in Davis than in the other communities. But, Table 5.8 shows that the price of constant quality, new housing was 33 per cent in Davis and 24 per cent in the other communities. This means that the comparative quality of new housing has decreased in Davis after the introduction of the GMP (Zorn et al. 1986: 54).

Table 5.8 Percentage increase in the predicted price of housing after the introduction of growth control.

Community	Constant quality housing	
	New housing prices	Old housing prices
Davis	38	28
Woodland	25	32
Roseville	20	24
Rancho Cordova	28	32
AVERAGE FOR CONTROL COMMUNITIES	24	30

Source: Zorn et al. (1986: 46-57).

After the implementation of the GMP, the sales price of old housing in Davis increased by 29 per cent while in the control communities it only increased by 22 per cent. But when one looks at all constant quality housing, Davis prices increased by 28 per cent and the control communities increased by 30 per cent. Thus, the quality of old housing in Davis has improved as compared to the other communities (Zorn et al. 1986: 55).

Zorn et al. (1986) then examine the change in affordability, using the same measure as Schwartz, Hansen and Green (1984)

In new housing the percentage decline in the proportion of new houses affordable to households earning 80% of median income was less in Davis than in the control communities (83% versus 96%). For households earning 120% of median income, the percentage decline in the proportion of new houses affordable in Davis and the control communities was approximately equal (55% versus 52%) (Zorn et al. 1986: 55-6).

In the old housing market, affordability for households earning 80 per cent of the median income declined by 89 per cent in Davis and by 72 per cent in the other communities. For those earning 120 per cent of median income, the percentage was 56 per cent versus 33 per cent. "In Davis the decline in affordable housing (new and old) for households earning 80% and 120% of median income was 86% and 56%, respectively, while the comparable decline in the control communities was 79% and 39%""(Zorn et al. 1986: 56). Thus, the price mitigation measures have arguably shifted some of the impacts of growth control from the new to the old housing market. Moreover, affordable housing is declining even with the measures aimed at producing affordable housing.

Niebanck (1989) examined the GMP of Santa Cruz, California, which is a system that aggressively reduces both the supply of developable raw land and the density of development on the remaining developable land. In 1975, the Housing Advisory Committee and the planning staff for the city of Santa Cruz prepared a report that estimated the local demand for housing and that proposed methods for satisfying the demand. In an effort to minimize the costs and maximize the benefits of growth, the report pinpointed the locations for, and densities of, future housing (Niebanck 1989: 108-9). The plan intended to reduce sprawl without slowing population growth.

In 1978, the citizens of Santa Cruz passed a strict growth control initiative. The initiative withdrew two "expansion" areas, amounting to approximately 1,000 acres, from residential designation. The initiative also cut the carrying capacity in half for 15 smaller "special" areas that totalled almost 500 acres.

Niebanck summarizes the impact of the initiative on available building sites as follows:

In 1975, Santa Cruz City had identified its vacant land housing carrying capacity, conservatively estimated, at 10,650 units. About three-fourths of these, or 7,600 units, were to have been located in certain small and large open areas called 'special' and 'expansion' areas. The balance was to have been absorbed in random lots of various sizes within the otherwise fully developed areas of the city. The passage and administration of growth control legislation has reduced the carrying capacity to 5,750 units. No housing is now permitted in the expansion areas, and the special areas will absorb only 2,400 units. The city later further down-zoned 10 of the 15 special areas (Niebanck 1989).

Santa Cruz County has also acted aggressively to curb growth. The county has used such methods as refusing to extend utilities, restricting land divisions, enforcing very low rural densities and aggressively acquiring open space. Niebanck compares the sales prices of existing housing stock in Santa Cruz County and in "comparison areas" during the decade of growth control. He estimates that, conservatively, "growth controls have added 10 per cent to the cost of existing houses in Santa Cruz County" (Niebanck 1989: 114–15).

All these studies show a correlation between the introduction of GMPs and increases in land and housing prices. Zorn et al. (1986) also show a correlation between the introduction of GMPs and reductions in the proportions of affordable housing both in Davis itself and in nearby local housing markets. Correlation is not the same as causality. What the information summarized so far does not explain is what causes these generally acknowledged increases in land and housing prices.

Local oligopolies and increases in land and housing prices

In order to explain the increases in price it is necessary to consider both the supply of developable land which GMPs restrict and the demand for that land. The interactions of the two together are what determines the market price of land. Planning authorities cannot usually cause the price of developable land to rise on their own. Planning authorities, having set the rules, can then only wait to react to proposals from developers. It is the interaction between developers and the rules established by planning authorities, in different local housing markets, that must be examined to seek explanations for rises in land and house prices. The following studies show that it is the development of oligopolies of large building firms within local housing markets, partly as a result of the establishment of GMPs, which explains the rises in land and, subsequently, in housing prices.

Landis (1986) examines the impact of growth limitation policies on housing prices in the California housing markets of San Jose, Sacramento County and Fresno. Just as Dowall, Landis (1986) argues that policies that restrict land availability can directly increase prices. Moreover, such policies can allow relatively few builders to dominate the market and further increase prices.

Landis points out that the earlier studies are predominantly descriptive. The descriptive nature of these studies is largely attributable to the fact that "we lack a usable theory with which to analyze the behaviour of actual housing markets""(Landis 1986: 9). According to Landis, housing economists simply presume that producers of new housing operate in a highly competitive market. "Accordingly, any and all housing price increases that exceed external cost increases can arise only from problems in the housing credit market or from local restrictions on the supply of housing" (Landis 1986)

Landis questions this widely accepted position and instead "suggests that in growing markets the most important price effects of local land-use controls are indirect, and that the structure of the local home-building industry influences how local regulations increase new home prices" (Landis 1986: 9–10).

Landis described the similarities and differences of San Jose, Sacramento County and Fresno as follows:

The three case-study areas are roughly comparable with regard to recent growth rates in population, housing, and employment. Where they differ is in the stringency of their controls on residential development. At one extreme is San Jose, which has aggressively pursued policies aimed at containing urban sprawl and encouraging "infill" development. Sacramento lies at the other, less regulated pole; during the late 1970s, Sacramento planners and politicians consciously adopted land development policies aimed at accommodating residential growth (Johnston et al. 1984). Between those two poles is the Fresno area. Since the

71

adoption of its 1975 General Plan, the city of Fresno has imposed increasingly strict controls on production home-building (Landis 1986: 10).

Landis also points out that between 1975 and 1980, the average size of a new home increased from 1,458 sq. ft to 1,850 sq. ft in Fresno. New homes in San Jose increased in size by a similar amount. In Sacramento, new homes only increased in size by approximately 100 sq. ft. Rather than ignoring increases in square footage as Schwartz et al. (1984) did with Petaluma, Landis attempts to determine "To what extent . . . housing price inflation, housing size inflation, and stringent controls on the availability of developable land are correlated" (Landis 1986: 11).

Although San Jose did experience a sharp increase in the price of raw land between 1972 and 1979, the Urban Service Boundary, however, did not by itself cause the inflation. San Jose was the last urban area in Santa Clara County that still had large tracts available. As San Jose came to be seen as a "hot" market, large builders from southern California and Canada came in and quickly bid up the prices. While the Urban Service Boundary did not start the bidding war, it did compound the price inflation by reducing the supply of developable land (Landis 1986: 12).

According to conventional wisdom, home builders are supposed to operate in competitive markets because there are no effective barriers to entry. Even if new firms were somehow prevented from entering the market, existing builders should not be able to exercise monopoly power because the buyers could turn to the supply of existing housing.

This view may no longer be accurate. As land prices increase, so it becomes more difficult for new builders to enter the market, especially if existing builders warehouse land at much lower prices. Moreover, as new homes become larger and packed with amenities, older homes no longer provide a satisfactory substitute (Landis 1986: 13).

In order to test the hypothesis that builders can influence the price of land, Landis divides housing markets into four categories. These are:
(a) competitive;
(b) contestable;
(c) noncontestable;
(d) closed.

In a competitive market, only efficient firms survive. As each home-builder attempts to find a niche, new homes will be provided at the lowest price possible over the entire range of housing sizes and qualities. Builders will not be able to seek higher profits simply by building larger houses and causing house size inflation because other builders will step in and supply the buyers with smaller houses (Landis 1986: 14).

In contestable markets, new builders may have to overcome sizeable entry costs. Once entry has been gained, new builders will be able to compete with existing builders. Thus, existing builders should not be able to raise prices any higher than the cost of entry. One potential impact of higher cost of entry could be the elimination of lower priced units (Landis 1986: 14–15).

In noncontestable markets, existing builders enjoy substantial input cost advantages over potential entrants, but new entrants have no exceptional entry costs. Thus, existing builders will always be able to build houses at a lower cost than new entrants. According to Landis, noncontestable markets have a rather interesting structure:

> Because entry is so infrequent, the structure of the home-building industry is extremely stable . . . and incumbents may learn to act strategically, incorporating the practices of their competitors into their own project planning . . . There will tend to be less competition: new firms may be discouraged from entering noncontestable markets, new home prices may be higher, and the market is likely to be segmented (that is, each firm will control a certain price and quality segment of the whole new home market). Noncontestable markets also will be characterized by a greater rate of size inflation (Landis 1986: 15).

In closed markets, new builders are faced with both sizeable entry costs and input cost differentials. In such cases, existing builders may segment the market; thus, there would be a lack of competition and high prices at every quality level (Landis 1986: 15).

Landis defines Sacramento as a competitive market, where local builders operate along side national builders. Table 5.9 shows that by 1981 the largest eight firms supplied 58 per cent of the local housing market. No single firm was able to dominate the market. Furthermore,

Sacramento seemed to operate as predicted. Homes were provided in a wide range of prices and sizes. The market was not segmented. Size inflation was negligible. Finally, the cost per sq. ft in Sacramento was lower than in both Fresno and San Jose, as shown in Table 5.10 (Landis 1986: 16). Apparently the Sacramento market is competitive because land is not scarce and thus there are no barriers to entry.

Table 5.9 Market share estimates for the single-family homebuilding industry. San Jose, Sacramento and Fresno markets, 1976–81.

Markets	Market share				
	1976	1977	1978	1980	1981
Sacramento (competitive)					
Largest eight firms (%)		40			58
Housing starts		9,000			2,500
San Jose (contestable)					
Largest eight firms (%)	58		69		81
Housing starts	5,221		3,595		953
Fresno (noncontestable)					
Largest eight firms		68		77	
Housing starts		1,900		950	

Source: Adapted from Landis (1986: 9–21).

Landis identifies three major entry costs in San Jose, which make it a contestable market these are:

(a) very high raw land costs;
(b) significant locally assessed construction and impact fees as well as potentially lengthy project reviews;
(c) the use of union labour was almost unavoidable due to the level of union activism in the area (Landis 1986: 16).

San Jose showed signs of behaving as a contestable market according to Landis's definition. Very high land prices drove some well known builders of low-cost homes from the market. As a consequence, new homes also became larger and more expensive (Table 5.10).

Fresno is identified as a noncontestable market because the urban limit line creates a dual land market due to the pattern of land ownership when it was implemented. Fresno builders are well established in the community. More importantly, they have consistently warehoused large tracts of land, buying them five or more years before they actually

Table 5.10 Comparison of new and existing single-family homes, San Jose, Sacramento and Fresno markets, 1975 and 1980

Markets and characteristics	Single-family homes			
	New homes		Existing homes	
	1975	1980	1975	1980
Sacramento (competitive)				
Sale price ($000)	45	83	38	67
Average square footage	1,530	1,620	1,450	1,450
Average price per sq ft ($)	30	52	26	51
San Jose (contestable)				
Sale price ($000)	54	130	45	108
Average square footage	1,650	1,800	1,387	1,400
Average price per sq ft ($)	33	72	32	77
Fresno (noncontestable)				
Sale price ($000)	na	99	na	64
Average square footage	1,458	1,850	na	1,370
Average price per sq ft ($)	na	54	na	47

Source: Adapted from Landis (1986: 9–21).

intended to develop them. First, this allowed existing builders to develop on land which they bought at extremely low prices. Secondly, existing builders tended to control much of the land within the urban fringe area, where development was being allowed. Thus, new builders were barred from entry into this market (Landis 1986: 18).

Although infill parcels were available, they were evidently more expensive and smaller, both of which raised input costs. In 1981 the eight largest builders controlled 81 per cent of Fresno's new home market (Table 5.9). Furthermore, almost all of the firms operating in Fresno were local. Finally, Fresno builders were able to segment the market and to increase the size of the houses (Landis 1986: 18).

Dowall (1984) also shows the importance of large building firms in determining the price of land and housing in Santa Rosa and Fremont. He argues that land prices can be driven up by market characteristics (who is buying and what is available) as well as by government interventions.

Santa Rosa, for example, was designated an Urban Growth Boundary in 1978. It was not trying to slow growth, but instead to make the delivery of services more affordable by halting leap-frog development.

After the city's designation, several builders outside the boundary were denied water and sewer services. Even though there was enough raw land within the boundary to meet Santa Rosa's housing needs through the year 2000, the price of land within the boundary quickly increased (Dowall 1984: 116). Large builders evidently bid up the price so that they would not get frozen out of the market.

Dowall's findings in Fremont also seem to support the conclusion that demand by large builders can be more important than the immediate demand of home buyers. In 1979, Fremont had plenty of land to develop, but very few of the large tracts – those of 50 acres or more and favoured by large developers – were available. Consequently, the Fremont prices were higher than one would expect from the demand for housing (Dowall 1984: 112).

Dowall also points out that developers can obtain monopoly power without cornering the entire market. Houses are not widgets. The size of the house and lot, the quality of the neighbourhoods and schools, the natural settings, the access to transportation and many other factors can combine to create small markets which a single developer can dominate. Land-use regulations help to create monopolies when they limit the supply of buildable land and make it easier for a single builder to control the supply. Land-use regulations can also favour large builders over small ones. By shifting the cost of extending public services to the developer, a local government increases the initial outlay for the developer. The increased entry cost may keep smaller developers out of the market and make it easier for the large developers to obtain monopoly power (Dowall 1984: 139–41).

In Marin County, for example, where land prices have always been high due to the unique natural environment, low residential densities and easy access to San Francisco, the county and cities aggressively reduced the supply of land through agricultural zoning, large lot zoning, a water hook-up moratorium, the acquisition of open space, and anti-growth annexation policies. Between 1975 and 1979, land prices in both San Rafael and Novato (Marin's two major cities) rose at an annual rate of 20–25 per cent. Dowall argues that these increases are largely due to land-use regulations.

In contrast, in Napa, where small builders predominate, the establishment of a residential urban line did not notably increase the price of land (Dowall 1984: 116). Smaller builders did not need to warehouse land and compete for large tracts. Instead, they could choose from many smaller parcels. Thus, the characteristics of the developers in a particular market might be a major factor influencing land prices.

Economic growth

Introduction

According to Hall et al. (1973) the second economic consequence of planning in Britain is that the rate of economic growth has probably been reduced. This is one of the results of planning predicted by Friedman (1962, Friedman & Friedman 1980). The imposition of planning controls in Britain has inhibited the spread of manufacturing industry into the suburbs and the countryside. The guardians of suburban and rural amenity have prevented this. Thus amenity has been traded off against economic growth.

This has not been the case in California. Before 1971 zoning and general plans did not have to be coordinated. Exclusionary zoning did not prevent the spread of industry, wholesale and retail outlets into the suburbs. Its main function was to separate industrial land-uses from others and not to restrict them to central urban areas. After the passage of Proposition 13 in 1978, many cities and counties positively encouraged motor car dealers, shopping malls and the like into their suburban areas in order to increase the local governments' revenue from sales tax.

Planning restrictions on the land available for economic developments have not been particularly severe in California. Any direct reduction in economic growth as a result of planning has therefore not been caused by non-existent or weak containment policies. Instead, economic growth may have been slowed by the direct imposition of extra costs on all kinds of development as a direct result of:
(a) delays;

(b) fees;

(c) agreements.

These were imposed by the planning system itself. The direct extra costs of planning imposed on development, and therefore potentially reducing the rate of economic growth, have been examined by Dowall (1984) and Delafons (1990).

Planning delays

Dowall's (1984) analysis of the extra costs imposed on, for example, housing development by local planning begins by pointing out that inflation has been the main factor driving up the cost of completed construction projects. Persistent inflation raises the cost of delay. So, if planning increases the delay between the purchase of raw land and the completion of construction this increases the cost of that construction. Dowall (1984) shows that planning in the San Francisco Bay Area has indeed delayed the completion of construction projects and therefore increased their cost.

As part of the increase in growth and environmental controls, builders have experienced lengthy review periods which have added considerably to the cost of development. According to Dowall, the review process may take as little as two months or as long as three years (Dowall 1984: 122). This is despite the fact that California passed the Permit Streamlining Act which requires local governments to approve or disapprove project applications within specified time periods. Part of the problem with this act, however, is that the courts decided, in *Landi vs County of Monterey* (1983), that the act does not apply to a local government's exercise of its legislative powers. Consequently, if a project requires a general plan amendment or a rezoning, the local government is not bound by any time schedule. Moreover, if litigation becomes a factor, the project might be held up for another two years. Finally, citizen opposition during the review process can add to the review period and eventually kill a project, provided that the project requires a legislative action (Frieden 1979).

Dowall identifies four factors that can add to the review period:

(a) if more than one agency reviews the application;

(b) if an environmental impact report (EIR) is required, the project can take much longer (EIRs are more often required for large projects);

(c) in most cases when developers attempt to use planned districts, which are designed to allow flexibility, innovation and the preservation of usable open space, the review process is longer than when conventional zoning is relied on;

(d) staff workloads greatly increase review time; since the passage of Proposition 13, local budgets and staffing levels have declined; thus, workloads have increased greatly (Dowall 1984: 123).

Any delays increase costs in four ways:

(a) by additional land-related costs (land interest costs, property taxes, overhead rates);

(b) by development loan interest costs;

(c) by inflation costs;

(d) by costs of capital tie-up (Dowall 1984: 125).

Table 5.11 shows the length of delay which these factors caused in five cities in the San Francisco Bay Area during 1978/9. It shows that delays varied from between 3 months for projects of less than ten housing units in Concord and Santa Rosa, up to more than 24 months for projects of more than 100 units in Fremont.

Table 5.11 Subdivision map approval periods (delay in months) for the San Francisco Bay Area, 1978/79.

Cities	Project size Number of housing units			
	< 10	10–25	25–100	> 100
Fremont	4–6	6–12	12–18	> 24
Concord	3	3–6	na	na
Santa Rosa	3	3–6	6–8	na
Napa	3–4	na	na	na
Novato	< 6	6–8	12	na

Source: Adapted from Dowall (1984: 152, Table 23).

Having identified the length and causes of planning delays, Dowall (1984) went on to attempt to estimate their direct costs to developers. Normally these costs would be passed on to home buyers by the construction companies when the homes were sold. Dowall used the following method to estimate the possible costs of delays in approval:

I assumed that home builders obtain construction loans only after all relevant local government approvals have been given. . . . For sample single-family housing proposals of ten, thirty, and fifty units, I have assumed minimum approval periods of four, eight, and twelve months, respectively, with the builders coordinating their planning and financing activities accordingly. . . . Raw land costs at the time of acquisition are assumed to be $10,000 per unit, and interest charges on the land acquisition loans an average of 12 per cent per year. Inflation is pegged at 10 per cent, and construction costs are estimated to be $95,000 per unit. . . . The property tax rate is $4.36 per $100 assessed property valuation. . . . and the homes take nine months to complete (Dowall 1984: 27).

Table 5.12 gives estimates of how much construction costs would increase if the time for approval is doubled. For 10-unit projects, a delay of four extra months would add about $4,000 or 3.4 per cent to the cost of construction. In a 50-unit development, a delay of one extra year would add roughly $12,000 or 10.2 per cent to the cost of construction.

Table 5.12 Effects of approval delays on new home construction costs (per unit costs; US$).

Cost item	Ten-unit project delay		Fifty-unit project delay	
	None	4 months	None	12 months
Land	10,000	10,000	10,000	10,000
Interest on land loan	400	800	1,200	2,400
Construction costs	95,000	98,150	95,000	104,500
Interest on construction loan	7,900	8,175	7,950	8,750
Fees	2,300	2,300	2,300	2,300
Additional property tax	0	150	0	450
TOTAL	115,600	119,575	116,450	128,400
Additional cost % attributable to delay		3.4		10.2

Source: Adapted from Dowall (1984: 125, Table 24).

Dowall found that inflation accounted for roughly 85 per cent of the increased cost due to delay. But, during much of the 1980s, the estimate of 10 per cent inflation would have been unrealistically high.

Finally, after adding together all of the four planning factors that increased housing costs:

(a) increased land costs;

(b) more stringent subdivision regulations;

(c) delays;

(d) increased hook-up charges.

Dowall estimated that land-use regulation increased the cost of housing by 18-34 per cent which, in 1979, was between $18,000 and $31,000. These calculations are shown in Table 5.13.

Table 5.13 Combined direct cost effect estimates of local land-use controls and fees on new housing (%).

Cost components	Additional cost	
	Low	High
Land	5	10
Subdivision improvements	5	10
Delay costs	4	10
Fees and charges	4	4
TOTAL	18	34

Source: Dowall (1984: 133, Table 26).

Development impact fees

The second major direct cost of planning that may reduce rates of local economic growth is development impact fees. These are also part of local government's response to funding limitations imposed by Proposition 13. Since the end of the 1970s, local governments have increasingly imposed development impact fees.

Before the 1980s, large builders would provide on-site services including local estate roads, hook-ups to water mains and sewers. The public sector supplied the off- site infrastructure and public facilities such as off-site road improvements, increases in water supply or sewage capacity, traffic lights, parks and expansion of schools. As public funds became scarcer, and as residents became more concerned about rapid growth, cities began to shift costs to the builder, usually through the development impact fee. Some cities have even required office developers to contribute to the provision of public transportation, low-income housing and child-care facilities (Delafons 1990: 2; Keating 1986: 133–4).

The imposition of development impact fees creates both an economic growth and an equity issue. As far as the latter is concerned, before Proposition 13, when residents moved into the community off-site infrastructure improvements and public facility expansions were paid for by the entire community through property taxes. Since Proposition 13 and the introduction of impact fees, many people argue that they treat new residents unfairly (Delafons 1990: 49).

The most important restraint on impact fees is the "reasonable nexus" test. Essentially, the courts demand that there be a clear relationship between the facility that the developer is being asked to provide, or contribute to, and the development that he will build (Delafons 1990: 26). Being the United States, the rational nexus test is not applied uniformly throughout the country. Delafons provides the following example:

> In Illinois the Courts require that the purpose for which the fee is to be charged is "specifically and uniquely attributable" to the development that gives rise to the fee. The Californian Courts, on the other hand, have adopted a much more liberal or flexible approach and require only that there should be a "reasonable relationship" between the facility to be provided and the development in question. As a result, impact fees . . . have flourished more in California than in any other state (Delafons 1990: 26–7).

Development agreements

The third and final planning cost that affects local economic growth is the linked action surrounding vested development rights and development agreements. It should be noted that Californian development agreements are not the same as planning agreements in Britain.

As a general rule, property owners in the United States do not have a "vested" or automatic right to develop their land consistently with the existing land-use regulations. In other words, local governments can change the zoning and general plan designations for property. In fact, local governments have been allowed to change the laws governing the use of land even after the developer had received preliminary approvals and spent large sums of money.

The seminal example of such planning action came to the courts as *Avco Community Developers, Inc.* vs *South Coast Regional Commission* (17 Cal.3d 785 (1976). In this case, the developer had already acquired several thousand acres and final map approval for a planned community development. The developer, however, had not acquired any building permits. Avco completed construction of storm drains, culverts, street improvements, utilities and other subdivision improvements. Then California passed the California Coastal Zone Conservation Act, which required Avco to obtain further permits before commencing construction of buildings.

Avco argued that, because it had already spent approximately $2 million on subdivision improvements, it should not have to receive any additional discretionary approvals. The California Supreme Court ruled that Avco had failed to meet the traditional vested rights common law rule, which states that a landowner does not have a vested right in any zoning of his or her property until he or she performs substantial work in good faith relying upon a building permit.

The decision in *Avco* ignored the realities of modern land development, which requires extensive land improvements before building permits can be secured. The dissatisfaction with *Avco* led to the passage of Assembly Bill 853 in 1978, which became known as the Development Agreement Statute (Sigg 1985: 704–5).

Development agreements are intended to put into the development process certainty for the developer and, as a consequence, they should lower rather than raise development costs (Sigg 1985: 705). The development agreement is a contract between the city or county and a developer enforceable by any of the parties. Unless the agreement provides otherwise, the applicable zoning, regulations and policies are those in force at the time of the execution of the agreement. While the developer gets certainty in the development process, the community often receives benefits back from the developer (Smith 1988: 277). Smith (1988) summarizes the effects of planning agreements as follows:

The primary benefit of the development agreement to the developer is to bind public agencies by contract to certain regulations governing a specific project at a given time. This allows the developer to proceed with the necessary expenditures of a project and to feel secure from local political, legal or fee changes or additional cost-incurring conditions or land dedications. The development agreements include more comprehensive project planning, the resolution of public service amenities desired by the city or county. Benefits to the public include lower housing costs through more efficient utilization of resources and more comprehensive planning. Other public benefits include parks, schools, water systems, sewers and fire stations (Smith 1988: 278).

In so far as Californian development agreements provide public facilities as a *quid pro quo* for some planning benefit to the developer, they bear some similarity to planning agreements in Britain.

Development agreements may also be used as planning tools. Local planners may use the agreement as a means to achieve a particular sequence of development and to ensure the construction of a desired mix of uses (Fulton 1989: 6).

While local governments have been able to extract greater concessions through development agreements than they would have through development exactions (Smith 1988: 282), there are some answered questions about the use of the agreements. Most importantly, development agreements may be an unconstitutional contracting away of the reserved police power (Fulton 1989: 6; Smith 1988: 283; Sigg 1985: 712–20). In most instances, "government may not contract away its right to exercise the police power in the future." (*United States Trust Co.* vs *New Jersey*, (431 US 1, 22 1976). Even though cities and counties have entered into over 500 development agreements since the law passed in 1979, the courts have yet to rule on the constitutionality of any of these contracts (Fulton 1989: 5).

The reserved police power question, however, is of more than academic interest. Development agreements have been used to head off opposition to projects by mooting the issue. For example, when slow-growth advocates have placed initiatives on the ballot, developers and public officials have repeatedly entered into development agreements before the election in a blatant attempt to undermine the reserved legislative power of the electorate (Fulton 1989: 9). If development agreements are unconstitutional, then existing city councils or boards of supervisors could not tie the hands of future elected officials or the voters. Citizens' groups have also complained that they have been locked out of the negotiation process (Fulton 1989: 6).

Although California was the first state to authorize the use of development agreements, similar enabling legislation has been enacted in Hawaii, Florida, Arizona, Nevada, Minnesota and Colorado. As yet none of these states has seen the fast proliferation of development agreements which California experienced (Fulton 1989: 6).

Residential and social segregation

Introduction

In Britain, the main social consequence of planning is the regressive distribution of physical environmental advantages and disadvantages, and also opportunities for the acquisition of wealth and income. The costs of environmental deterioration, increased housing and transport costs, and lower rates of capital appreciation of property values have been borne mainly by the urban underprivileged tenants of public housing and tenants in private rented property. The corresponding benefits in physical environments, value for money in housing and faster than average capital appreciation of house values have accrued mainly to middle-class ruralites and the new owner-occupier suburbanites (Hall et al. 1973). These results have been brought about mainly by residential and consequential social segregation.

In America, residential and social segregation reflect not only differences in income and wealth, but also racial differences. There, marked differences in where different status and racial groups live are the product of:
(a) housing finance;

(b) planning and zoning;

(c) the lack of major public housing programmes.

Different residential locations give rise to a whole range of differences in opportunities for access to income, wealth and externalities. Frequently underlying these differences, as in Britain, is a conscious and deliberate attempt to protect the private property values of existing and future private property owners.

Housing finance

The Federal Government has played a major part in housing finance and residential segregation in America. During the height of the Depression, in 1933, something like half of all home loans were technically in default (Jackson 1985: 193). This persuaded President Roosevelt to urge the Congress to establish the Home Owners Loan Corporation (HOLC). The HOLC refinanced tens of thousands of mortgages that were in danger of default. It also granted low-interest loans that permitted owners to repurchase their foreclosed homes (Jackson 1985: 196).

The HOLC "introduced, perfected, and proved in practice the feasibility of the long-term, self-amortising mortgage with uniform payments spread over the whole life of the debt" (Jackson 1985: 196). The long-term mortgage had never developed in the United States as it did in England (Hall 1988).

In the long term, the HOLC contributed to residential segregation because of the use made of its appraisal methods by other lenders, notably the Federal Housing Administration (FHA). The HOLC systematized appraisal methods. "With care and extraordinary attention to detail, HOLC appraisers divided cities into neighbourhoods and developed elaborate questionnaires relating to the occupation, income, and ethnicity of the inhabitants and the age, type construction, price range, sales demand, and general state of repair of the housing stock" (Jackson 1980: 85).

The system was based on four categories that allegedly corresponded to the stability of the neighbourhood. The categories had letters with corresponding colours as follows:

A was green. Green areas were new, racially and economically homogeneous, and in demand even in bad economic times. Homogeneous was defined as being occupied solely by "American business and professional men. Jewish neighbourhoods or even those with an infiltration of Jews could not be considered best" (Jackson 1985: 197).

B was blue. A blue designation was used when a neighbourhood was still desirable even though it had reached its peak (Jackson 1985: 197). At that time, Americans believed when a neighbourhood became "old", decline was inevitable. The blue neighbourhood's desirability, however, would ensure an extended period of stability despite the age of the neighbourhood.

C was yellow. Yellow neighbourhoods were seen as declining because of age, obsolescence, or change of style. The decline of these neighbourhoods reduced rents and prices to a level that attracted "undesirables" (Jackson 1985: 197).

D was red. These were known as "hazardous" areas. These were areas where "decline" and "undesirables" had firmly taken root. "Black neighbourhoods were invariably rated D, as were any areas characterized by poor maintenance, poverty, or vandalism" (Jackson 1985: 197–8).

The HOLC's appraisal system reflects what were already common assumptions in the United States about housing stock and neighbourhoods. These were:

(a) Decline of neighbourhoods was seen almost as a biological inevitability as the structures aged and became obsolete.

(b) As the housing stock declined, it would trickle down to families of lower and lower incomes.

(c) The influx of certain ethnic groups would create declines in real estate prices and, potentially, white flight (Jackson 1985: 198).

This third assumption underlies the early and continuing concern with private property values shown not only by the owners themselves, but also by lending and planning institutions.

The HOLC applied these assumptions to every major city in the nation. It literally assigned one of the four categories to every block in every city. The designations were recorded on secret "Residential Security Maps" kept in the local HOLC office (Jackson 1985: 199). Their major contribution to residential segregation arose from the adoption of the rating system by private lending institutions. Savings and loans as well as banks used the system simply to eliminate all C and D areas from consideration for mortgages. This practice has been called "redlining". Residential segregation became an underlying Federal Government policy when the HOLC appraisal methods, and perhaps the secret maps themselves, were adopted by FHA (Jackson 1985: 203).

The FHA hastened the decay of the city cores by making escape from the city easier for the middle class. In addition, the FHA money did not reach the city cores. The legislation favoured single-family projects because the terms for multi-family projects were not as favourable. Consequently, "Between 1941 and 1950, FHA-insured single family starts exceeded FHA multi-family starts by a ratio of almost four to one. In the next decade, the margin exceeded seven to one" (Jackson 1985: 206). This extreme bias necessarily favoured the suburbs at the expense of the cities.

Furthermore, the FHA loans for repairs of older structures were for small amounts and short durations; hence, it was easier to purchase a new home than to rehabilitate an older one (Jackson 1985: 206). The legislation was also biased against rental housing in that the FHA exercised greater control over such projects (Jackson 1985: 206).

Finally, FHA mortgages required an "unbiased professional estimate", which was an appraisal "that included a rating of the property itself, a rating of the mortgagor or borrower, and a rating of the neighbourhood" (Jackson 1985: 207). While the evaluation procedure was similar to that of HOLC, FHA applied the process in a way that favoured white suburbs and discriminated against mixed neighbourhoods.

The FHA did not stop with the segregation of uses. Instead, it openly endorsed the segregation of races. It feared that an entire area could lose its investment value if rigid white/black separation was not maintained. It warned that "If a neighbourhood is to retain stability, it is necessary that properties shall continue to be occupied by the same social and racial classes" (Jackson 1985: 208).

The net effects of American public and private home financing policies have been that, although a tremendous amount of housing was built between 1945 and 1970, the benefits of the suburbs had been predominantly reserved for the upper half of the income structure. The FHA system failed to serve the poor, single women and minorities. The FHA also failed to serve the working class and lower middle class, and white men who were older and no longer in the prime of their earning capacity (Hayden 1984: 55). The people who could not move to the suburbs because of income, religion, age, or colour were left to the cities and an ageing housing stock.

In terms of private property values, the earliest residents of the suburbs may have received the best deal, because the cost of new houses continually rose after the Second World War. Inflation was persistent; consequently raw materials and wages increased. Moreover, the wages of construction workers apparently increase faster than their productivity and the Consumer Price Index (CPI). The price of suburban land also rose faster than the CPI. The FHA reported that the price of new lots rose by nearly five times from 1946 to 1967 (Clawson & Hall 1973: 129). As a consequence, earlier buyers built up large amounts of equity. In the west and southwest, the value of suburban property increased at even faster rates during the 1970s and 1980s.

Planning and zoning

Cities also used planning zoning to segregate races and social classes. After the Second World War both relied on economic barriers instead of explicitly stated racial prohibitions. Again, underlying economic segregation was the desire to protect property values.

Those who moved out to the suburbs were set on protecting their investment. The new suburbanites had seen the incredible decline in property values in the cities which they themselves had helped to create. For example, the city of Newark, New Jersey, changed from a white, middle-class city to an impoverished black city with an abandoned industrial base in the space of a single decade. The change caused millions of dollars in property values to vanish (Ables 1989: 136). In order to protect their own property values, many suburbs adopted exclusionary zoning ordinances that required minimum lot sizes or minimum house sizes large enough to prohibit the construction of low- and moderate-income housing (Ables 1989: 145).

Certain states such as California, have taken some action to break down exclusionary zoning barriers. In California, when a developer agrees to make at least 25 per cent of a development low- or moderate-income units, or 10 per cent lower income units, or 50 per cent units for senior citizens, a city is required to provide a density bonus of at least 25 per cent greater than the normal maximum (California Government Code 65915–65918).

California also requires all cities and counties to include a housing element in their general plans. The housing element is intended to be a comprehensive assessment of current and projected housing needs for all economic groups (California Government Code 65302(c), 65580–65589.8). Housing need is based upon the community's fair share of the regional housing need. The fair share is initially determined by the council of governments (COG).

The housing element, however, is proving to be a paper tiger. Communities are not required to use the COG's determination. Instead, a community can use its own determination and supporting data. Furthermore, even though a community is required to identify potential housing sites for all income levels, the community is not required to find adequate sites and resources to meet the actual need. Stated differently, the sites identified may be inadequate to meet the actual need.

Moreover the community is not required to allow housing developments that are in sharp conflict with the remainder of the general plan. Thus open-space, agricultural, and large-lot general plan designations can still bar the construction of low-income housing. Case studies by the Stanford Environmental Law Society (1982) confirm that communities are using alleged environmental goals to avoid meeting the housing needs of lower income residents (Juelsgaard 1983: 136–40).

Large-lot zoning, open-space zoning and agricultural zoning have been used as parts of growth control programmes. Several studies have shown that growth controls can have inflationary impacts on housing prices that lead to the elimination of low- and moderate-priced housing (Dowall 1984, Schwartz et al. 1984).

Fischel (1985) argues that zoning, as it is now practised, allows communities to shift costs onto others, which in turn leads to over-regulation and densities that are too low:

> Communities can have a substantial impact on the overall density of population. The major reason is that courts of law are willing to sustain zoning laws . . . that substantially reduce the value of undeveloped land. This allows the community to reap the benefits of restrictive zoning (to current home-owners and other voters) without having to confront the cost that these regulations impose on developers and prospective residents. Non-market substitutes for compelling the community to account for costs of regulation are seldom required by the courts. Communities do not have to do anything approximating benefit-cost analysis before imposing land use regulations. This condition leads to over-regulation and residential densities that are too low (Fischel 1985: 65).

While it is difficult to achieve a statewide or regional measure of the impacts of exclusionary zoning, case studies have shown that, after the application of political pressure by citizens' groups, local governments have used large-lot zoning, open-space zoning and agricultural zoning to the detriment of low- and moderate-income families. Frieden (1979) shows how community opposition caused several projects to be modified in such a manner that housing prices increased substantially. Table 5.14 shows the reductions in housing numbers and the increases in housing prices after local opposition caused different projects to be scaled down in Mountain Village, Harbor Bay and Crocker Hills in the San Francisco Bay Area. It shows that, in all cases housing numbers were cut while both house sizes and prices were increased.

The decline of affordable housing as a result of the implementation of the first GMP in Petaluma, California, is also shown by Schwartz et al. (1984). They studied the GMP of Petaluma to find out what its effects were on the supply of low- and moderate-income housing.

Petaluma passed its innovative GMP in 1972 and gained national attention. The plan established a housing quota of 500 new units per year during the years 1973 through 1977. The quota applied to single-family detached and multi-family construction. The permits were to be allocated on a competitive basis, based on two major sets of criteria:

(a) The first required the developer to provide adequate public services.

91

(b) The second encouraged the construction of houses and subdivisions with a high level of amenities (Schwartz et al. 1984: 110–11).

Table 5.14 Changes to planned housing elements from affordable to expensive housing: Mountain Village, Harbor Bay and Crocker Hills, San Francisco Bay Area, 1972 to 1976.

Area		Plan dates			
		1972	1973	1974	1976
	Average price ($)	Housing units (nos)			
Mountain Village, Oakland					
Single-family rowhouses	40,000	23			
Single-family rowhouses	33,500	1,080			
Apartments	23,750	1,080			
TOTAL		2,183			
Lots for estate homes	35–75,000				100
Single-family rowhouses	40–60,000				150–200
TOTAL					200–300
Harbor Isle, Alameda					
Apartments	21–37,000	9,055			
TOTAL		9,055			
Single-family houses	38–57,500		4,385		
Two-family houses (duplex)	70,000		565		
TOTAL			4,950		
Single-family houses	55–165,000				3,170
TOTAL					3,170
Crocker Hills, San Mateo County					
Town houses and apartments	na		12,500		
TOTAL			12,500		
JUNE					
Town houses and apartments	33–60,000			9,690	
SEPTEMBER					
Town houses and apartments	40–70,000 31–48,000			7,655	
TOTAL				7,655	
ZONING APPROVAL					
Town houses and apartments	na				2,235
TOTAL					2,235

Source: Adapted from Frieden (1979).

The system unarguably lowered the level of growth in Petaluma. During the programme's first three years, "only 37% of the single-family units proposed by developers received allocations (permissions to build) and . . . the number of building permits issued was 67% less than the number issued during the three years before growth control" (Schwartz et al. 1984: 111).

In their study, Schwartz et al. attempted to find out the impact of Petaluma's GMP on the availability of moderately priced housing. They defined such houses as those affordable to moderate-income households, who in turn were defined as those households with an income between 80 per cent and 120 per cent of the county's median income for a household of four people.

Schwartz et al. used the city of Santa Rosa as a comparison city. Santa Rosa is to the north of Petaluma and had no permit allocation system, although it did implement an Urban Service Boundary. By using a comparison city, Schwartz et al. hoped to control for factors other than the GMP (Schwartz et al. 1984: 111).

According to Schwartz et al., the impact of the GMP has been dramatic. Tables 5.14 & 5.15 summarize the extremes of their results. Table 5.15 shows that new housing built for sale at less than $20,000 disappeared in Petaluma by 1976. In Santa Rosa it declined but still remained at 11 per cent in 1976. New housing built for sale at less than $35,000 declined from 100 per cent to 75 per cent in Petaluma while it remained in the 70 per cent range in Santa Rosa.

The change in housing stock was attributed in part to the competitive point system for issuing permits. Over 50 per cent of the maximum number of points awarded were for architectural design quality, site design quality, character of landscaping and screening, provision of foot paths, bicycle paths and equestrian trails, and the provision of usable open space (Schwartz et al. 1984: 112). Only 15 points out of a total of 130 were awarded for the provision of affordable housing (Schwartz et al. 1984: 114). More modest developments were quickly eliminated from the competition.

Table 5.16 shows that, unlike in Britain, house sizes increased after the introduction of development restrictions. In Petaluma new houses of less than 1,200 sq. ft declined from 20 to 1 per cent of the total between 1970 and 1976. Even houses of less than 1,900 sq. ft declined from 81 to 40 per cent of the total. In Santa Rosa, in contrast, both categories increased from 5 to 16 per cent for those under 1,200 sq. ft, and from 71 to 81 per cent for those under 1,900 sq. ft.

Table 5.15 Distribution of sales prices of new houses. Cumulative percentage of houses sold at or below the stated price, Petaluma and Santa Rosa, 1970 and 1976.

Sale price < $	Cumulative percentage			
	Petaluma		Santa Rosa	
	1970	1976	1970	1976
20,000	9	0	26	11
35,000	100	75	79	74

Source: Adapted from Schwartz et al. (1984: 110–14, Table 1).

Table 5.16 Distribution of floor area of new houses. Cumulative percentage of houses whose floor area is at or below the stated size (sq. ft): Petaluma and Santa Rosa, 1970 and 1976.

Floor area < sq. ft	Cumulative percentage			
	Petaluma		Santa Rosa	
	1970	1976	1970	1976
1,200	20	1	5	16
1,900	81	40	71	81

Source: Adapted from Schwartz et al. (1984: 110–14, Table 2).

Miller (1986) criticizes the study of Schwartz et al. for focusing only on new, single-family, detached housing. Miller argues that one can still have moderately priced housing in a new multi-family market and in the resale market. The shift to multi-family dwellings should be welcomed because increased densities reduce the consumption of land and the cost of delivering services. Miller also faults Schwartz et al. for statistically removing changes in the type of houses sold so that price fluctuations could be attributed solely to the GMP (Miller 1986: 319). Nevertheless, even with these caveats in mind it would have taken a radically different points system to induce developers to supply more affordable housing in Petaluma, a situation very much against local residents' wishes – they simply wanted to protect their own existing property values.

Other studies in California, such as those by Niebanck (1989) in Santa Cruz and Coyle (1983) in Palo Alto, have all argued that the effect of planning restrictions on growth has been to reduce the availability of affordable housing. In doing so, they also increase the degree of residential segregation based on ability to pay. Existing residents clearly understand that this can be an effective strategy to pursue with the local planning authority in order to maintain the value of their own houses.

The lack of major public housing programmes

In America there is no possibility that a lack of affordable housing and residential segregation will be remedied by public housing programmes. This is because:

(a) the programmes have always been minute by European standards;
(b) one of their peculiarities is that they can only be implemented by destroying old affordable but slum housing;
(c) as in Britain, such programmes have been decimated during the 1980s.

The American government has never produced public housing on the same scale as European countries. First of all, public housing in the United States has always been limited to the poor, except for extraordinary circumstances, such as housing provided for armament factory workers in the Second World War.

Secondly, public housing has never amounted to more than a tiny fraction of the housing stock. Publicly owned and operated housing only accounts for approximately 1 per cent of the US housing stock (Keating et al. 1990: 207). In addition to these units, the government has subsidized another 1.9 million privately owned low-income units. The government also issues approximately 800,000 rent subsidies (Keating et al. 1990: 207).

Although 2 million subsidized units may seem a considerable number, one should remember that even back in 1980 the USA had 88.4 million housing units (Adams 1987: 5). Consequently, public housing programmes have had little impact on the entire housing stock, especially when compared with the FHA programmes which financed private home ownership. Nevertheless, public housing programmes have played an important rôle in shaping cities and particularly ghettos in America.

The local participation requirement was broadened in 1949. The bottom line was that municipalities had control over when and where public housing could be built. Local control ensured racial segregation and the re-enforcement of inner-city poverty (Jackson 1985: 225). Local control also denied public housing access to the cheaper land in the suburbs (Jackson 1985: 225). Even when cities accepted low-income public housing, typically it was restricted to the non-white, impoverished neighbourhoods.

While the segregation of races in projects has been well documented, a perverse aspect of the housing programme was that, by intent, it could not increase the supply of housing. For each unit of public housing built, one slum unit had to be eliminated. The explanation for the one-unit-destroyed-for-each-unit-built requirement is that the programme became largely a slum clearance programme. In order to garner the support of local civic leaders, slums had to be cleared to boost the sagging tax structure and, again, to increase property values (Jackson 1985: 225–6).

The Federal public housing policy repeatedly changed during the late 1960s through to the late 1980s. These changes were initially due to a recognition that the inner cities had reached a state of crisis. Later changes were brought about by the Reagan administration's goal of removing the Federal Government from the public housing business.

When unrest erupted in the cities in the late 1960s, government responded by increasing housing assistance. The Department of Housing and Urban Development (HUD) was also established as a cabinet level position. This eliminated the FHA. "The Housing and Urban Development Act of 1968 increased federal aid for public housing and established programmes for interest rate subsidies for low-income home ownership . . . and rent subsidies to stimulate construction of multi-family rental housing. . . . Between 1969 and 1970 the share of all housing starts subsidized by the federal government more than doubled, jumping from 12% to 25%" (Lilley 1980). "Approximately as many public housing units were constructed in the 6–year period between 1968 and 1973 as were constructed over the 19–year period between 1949 and 1967, and operating subsidies for public housing increased over a hundredfold from 1969 to 1982" (Bratt 1986; quoted in Marshall & Florida 1990: 40–1).

This surge in activity, however, was short-lived. In 1980 the Reagan administration embarked on a strategy designed to remove the Federal Government from the low-income housing business.

Specific objectives included completely privatizing federally supported mortgage markets . . . substituting housing vouchers for new construction, tightening eligibility requirements, eliminating programmes, at least partially privatizing the existing stock of public housing, and, most important, drastically reducing federal spending on housing. Budget authority for subsidized housing, which peaked at $31.5 billion in 1978, fell to $13.3 billion in 1982 and $9.5 billion in 1987. . . . Nonfederal sources of new low-income housing construction were virtually eliminated by changes to federal tax laws in 1986; tax incentives, the major attraction for private investors, for constructing new low-income housing through either direct investment or tax-exempt Industrial Development Bonds were virtually eliminated. By the late 1980s, the federal government had essentially abandoned its commitment to housing assistance (Marshall & Florida 1990: 40–1).

Although some states and private lenders have taken steps to bridge the affordability gap, these programmes tend to be aimed at moderate-income white families, the same people who initially benefited from FHA (Marshall & Florida 1990; 42). Thus, the poor minorities and elderly persons, who were the beneficiaries of the government housing programmes of the 1960s and 1970s, have been left out in the cold.

To an extent, nonprofit Community Development Corporations (CDCs) have stepped in to provide low-income housing. Many CDCs were initiated in the decade between 1965 and 1975, a period when Federal, foundation and corporate assistance were available to support CDC housing projects (Keating et al. 1990: 210). When Reagan took office, however, the modest Federal support for CDCs was drastically reduced

(Keating et al. 1990: 211). While some private philanthropic foundations as well as state and local governments have increased their contributions to CDCs, such contributions have not made up for the loss of federal support for low-income housing (Keating et al. 1990: 221).

Summary and conclusions

The guiding principles of the Californian planning system are the protection and enhancement of the rights of private property owners and limited intervention in development markets. This is not to say that every individual planning action takes one or both of these forms. This is because, just as most public policies, it is a system responding to mutually incompatible, external conflicts of interest. In the case of planning these conflicts are between private versus public interests; private individuals versus public institutions; private property rights versus public regulation; and between markets and plans. These conflicts pull the system in different directions. The outcomes at any particular point in time depend upon the balance of forces in contention over particular issues.

The protection and enhancement of the rights of private property owners, and limited intervention in development markets, come to be the most common guiding principles of the Californian planning system, because private property owners and large-scale developers are the best equipped and organized to obtain these outcomes from the conflicts surrounding planning. They do not always win all the individual conflicts and this is why not every individual planning action results in the protection and enhancement of the rights of private property owners and limited intervention in development markets. The majority, however, do take one or other of these forms.

These major characteristics of the Californian planning system are the reasons why it is used in this study as a base line from which to compare the effects of planning in Britain.

One major distinguishing feature of Federal and Californian planning policy is that there are no national or state policies for the containment of urban growth. In California there were no effective planning mechanisms which could have been used to contain urban growth before 1971 when state planning law was changed to require the coordination of general plans and zoning ordinances.

Attitudes towards and policies for local urban containment can be divided into two main periods. In the first period, lasting until the 1970s, there was little support for containment. One result of this was that millions of Americans were able to purchase relatively inexpensive and reasonably sized, single-family housing in the growing suburbs. As far as individual property owners were concerned this was a major benefit of having no general or effective policies for urban containment.

During the 1970s support began to grow not so much for containment as for limiting rates of local urban growth. This is expressed in the form of local initiatives for growth management policies. The effects of such policies have usually been to reduce the rate of growth of suburban single-family housing. But, the fiscalization of planning in California has meant that they have not reduced the rate of growth of commercial properties which provide sales tax revenues to hard-pressed local governments.

In general, GMPs only reduce the rate of local peripheral urban growth. They do not fix permanent limits to this growth in the way that, for example, Green Belts do in Britain. They are therefore not policies for absolute containment but for slower growth than would otherwise have been the case. It is not to be expected, therefore, that they will have such marked, if not extreme, effects as the absolute containment of cities in Britain by the rigid application of Green Belt policies.

Suburbanization is a process that has taken place without much planning in America. During earlier periods of suburbanization in California the separation of white-collar jobs from home was probably reduced. During this period employers were moving work to where suitable workforces already lived. These early moves divorced the location of work and housing from the older public transport systems and so made a growing number of journeys to work dependent on the private motor car and the public freeway system.

The growing problems of suburbanization have come with the continued growth of employment in the suburbs combined with public intervention in the supply of housing as a result of growth management policies and the enforcement of Proposition 13. This has led to a lack of new and affordable houses in those suburban locations where employment has been growing.

It is very difficult to link multiple suburban job locations with other suburban housing locations using public transport. The result is growing freeway congestion, lengthening journeys to work and increasing air pollution. Los Angeles and the San Francisco Bay Area are prime examples of these problems.

These complex relationships between the location of home and work and the regular journeys between them present a major challenge to Californian planners. It remains to be seen whether the predominance of private property rights and market forces will give way to any planned and rational solution to this problem.

Growth management policies are changing the conditions in local housing markets. These changes in the local rules of development do not by themselves increase the price of land and housing. They do seem to stimulate demand from larger building companies for large plots of developable land. Their demands, together with the warehousing of the larger plots of future development land, tends to force smaller firms out of the market and thereby decrease competition. This allows the remaining land holders and development firms to charge higher prices for those commodities than would be the case in fully competitive markets.

The most important underlying effect of GMPs is to make local property markets less competitive. Smaller numbers of larger firms come to dominate local housing markets. Thus, the major planning principle of limited intervention in development markets does not result in the maintenance of competitive markets. Instead, it encourages the establishment of oligopolistic (i.e. small numbers of larger firms) domination of local housing markets. These are not competitive markets. They are marked by characteristics which suit the interests of a few larger development firms. The small builders who had contributed to the building of the post Second World War suburbs have given way increasingly to the large building firms.

In California planning delays and development impact fees probably slow economic growth. On the other hand, development agreements between the larger firms and local planners probably smooth the path towards economic growth. The net balance of the effects of these policies on economic growth may be about neutral.

Planning delays and development impact fees increase the costs of development. In so far as increases in costs slow economic growth, then the effects of these planning actions probably serve to reduce rates of local economic growth in California.

On the other hand, development agreements seem to be an increasingly important way in which developers, particularly large developers, can secure favourable planning treatment for their future developments. Assuming that they are not ruled unconstitutional by the courts, they appear to be a way of reducing the costs imposed on developers by planning. They may be working in the opposite direction to delays and impact fees in so far as they reduce medium and long-term costs for developers and, therefore, do not tend to reduce the rate of economic growth.

The evidence on whether planning restricts economic growth in California is therefore mixed. Bearing in mind the guiding principles of the Californian planning system, which are the protection and enhancement of the rights of private property owners and limited intervention in development markets, it depends whether property owners increasingly push to trade some economic growth for better housing conditions and the response of large developers as to whether planning will restrict economic growth more in the future than it has done in the past.

In America, planning and zoning have combined with a discriminatory housing finance system and the lack of a significant public housing programme to spread different social and racial groups out over space. This has produced residential and social segregation. Its most extreme forms are racial segregation and the urban ghettos.

As far as planning is concerned, exclusionary zoning and growth management policies have served to segregate populations according to their different abilities to pay for housing in the market place. GMPs have tended to make housing relatively scarcer, more expensive and larger. All these factors make for increased residential and social segregation.

Residential segregation is important because of the differences in access to a wide range of both public and private goods and services that follows from where families are able to live. On the one hand some locations give access to clean environments, good schools, parks and other public and private benefits. Other locations trap those who cannot escape from them in unhealthy surroundings with minimal or non-existent public facilities. The arrangement of these locational differences and opportunities on the ground in terms of new land-uses and the built environment has, in the past, been a prime official concern of planning.

Underlying planning, financial and government programmes in California, however, is the objective of protecting existing land and property values. Financial appraisal systems, zoning ordinances, GMPs and other policies have all been supported by existing and potential private property owners. They do not see residential integration as a way of maintaining and enhancing their property values. For this reason and because of their political power in the conflicts over planning policies, residential integration is unlikely to become a major planning goal in California.

CHAPTER SIX
Relaxed and tough containment: Britain

Introduction

The post-war planning system was established with the broad objectives of containing urban areas and creating self-contained and balanced communities. Implicit in these objectives was the assumption that urban sprawl should be controlled and the loss of good agricultural land prevented, while self-contained new towns were to be established to accommodate future urban growth. These objectives brought together several strands of planning ideology, in particular the garden city movement which had stressed small-scale urbanization, accessibility to opportunities and environmental quality.

In practice, these objectives were highly conservative. As Hall et al. (1973) have suggested, they were based upon a notion of the guidance of change in the interest of social stability and continuity with the past. Cities, for instance, were to be controlled with Green Belts and fragmented into neighbourhood units to revive something akin to the village community.

The implementation of these policies varied according to changes in the political control of the central state and the economic context. Broadly speaking, it is possible to distinguish three phases of post-war planning. These are:

1 1947–68 was a period of economic growth during which many of the early planning schemes came to fruition. They were devised and implemented in an elitist and professional manner, with an emphasis on rationality, efficiency and aggregate improvement.

2 1969–78 was a time when economic decline set in and public dissatisfaction with some of the results of the earlier period led to political and economic challenges. Local government was reformed.

3 1979–91 was a period of overall economic decline in which planning has been attacked for interfering with economic growth by placing limits on the pace of development. Regional planning was weakened, metropolitan authorities were abolished, planning controls were loosened.

The first phase, particularly under the Labour administration which lasted from 1947 to 1951, saw a massive transfer of power from individuals to the state. As originally implemented via the Town and Country Planning Act 1947, this involved the limitation of the absolute right of landowners to develop land, with this right now becoming conditional on receiving the permission of the state. Development had a legal definition and its control was exercised by the newly created local planning authorities, generally the largest available local authorities, who were also charged with the task of preparing 20-year development plans outlining all important future developments and changes of land-uses. Planning permission for development was granted on the basis of development plan proposals or "other material considerations". The latter are not defined by the 1947 Act, nor any subsequent acts, and have generally been set by precedent to include factors such as central government policies, the aesthetics of the scheme and site considerations. The system is thus comprehensive in the sense of covering most forms of urban development but narrow in focusing primarily on land-use controls and not applying to agriculture, which is the major land use in Britain (Table 6.1)

As Ambrose (1986) has suggested, the introduction of this new planning legislation should be understood in the context of the national feeling pervasive during the Second World War of the need for radical changes in post-war society in order to reduce resented patterns of inequality, and thus give the masses something to fight for. However, this feeling rested upon great expectations of what could be achieved by such a planning system and the assumption that its actions could be defined in terms of the public interest.

Table 6.1 Land-use changes: England and Wales, 1933–63.

Category of use	1933	1963	Change	Change (%)	
	Million acres			Category[1]	National area[2]
Urban	2.7	4.0	1.3	49	4
Rural	34.6	33.3	−1.3	−6	−3
TOTAL	37.3	37.3			

Source: Adapted from Coleman (1977).
Notes:
1. Category change = area becoming urban as a percentage of land in urban use in 1933.
2. National area = area becoming urban as a percentage of total land in 1933.

During the second period, from 1969 to 1978, dissatisfaction with the system, resulting from discrepancies experienced by individual citizens between the visions promised by the early post-war plans and how they turned out in practice, led to reforms. In political terms, challenges arose as it was realized that there were gainers and losers in the planning process and that planning had distributional consequences. Davies (1972) and Dennis (1972) showed how many of the post-war development plans turned out to be nightmares for the citizens affected by them. As a result, citizen participation was formally introduced into the planning process after 1968. Following these critiques, planning lost much of its original innocence and was now open to much more explicit lobbying by pressure groups.

The planning system also received new challenges as the national and international economy moved into recession in the early 1970s. While the immediate post-war period had been one in which planning had operated to guide rapid growth, planning increasingly saw its rôle being recast to that of promoting growth almost at any cost. In particular, the 1970s were a period in which the capitalist economy entered into a downswing. The period was also one of major industrial restructuring as firms sought to rationalize and reorganize their operations in order to maintain profitability. This process has had dramatic effects on some localities, with the older inner cities in particular facing widespread dereliction and unemployment.

At the same time, newer production activities were taking root in places outside the former industrial areas. High-technology industries, for instance, have increasingly sought locations in high-amenity areas capable of attracting a highly qualified and highly paid workforce (Hall et al. 1987). Most frequently, these requirements have been met in non-metropolitan southeast England, often in areas most protected by post-war planning policies. This in turn has generated new conflicts for the planning system to resolve.

The period between 1979 and 1991 was one of overall economic decline in which planning was attacked for interfering with economic growth by placing limits on the pace of development. Regional planning was weakened, metropolitan authorities were abolished, planning controls were loosened. These constituted the most radical attacks on the 1947-style land-use planning system since it was introduced. At the time of writing in 1992, more radical changes to both the planning and local government systems are in the pipeline.

The issues introduced above and their subsequent effects are discussed in the same format as those for California. This allows, as far as possible, for direct comparisons between the effects of land-use planning in Britain and California with respect to containment, suburbanization, land and house prices, economic growth and residential segregation.

Containment

Introduction

The British system of land-use planning is based on conflicts between private-property interests, which favour the use of markets to decide the uses to which they can put their property, and public interests, which look to public institutions, regulation and plans to provide goods and services which markets characteristically do not. There are conflicts between different groups within these two large and general categories.

The history of British planning is one of elite and paternalistic decisions to introduce effective public regulation over land-uses in the name of the public interest. For a brief period during the 1970s public participation in planning decisions became fashionable. Since then, however, both public regulation and participation have been in decline in the face of economic problems and the re-assertion of market forces over plans.

The re-assertion of market forces in planning brings to the fore the basic contradiction on which the whole enterprise rests. This is the conflict between the drive to assist market forces to generate economic growth by providing infrastructure, information and other enabling functions, and the need to legitimate planning to the general public by acting in the public interest, encouraging public participation, establishing social objectives and generally assisting to create social harmony. It may be possible to follow both objectives during times of economic growth. The first objective has taken precedence during the 1980s. This is partly because of economic limitations and partly because of the ideological predisposition of the Conservative central government.

Despite assertions to the contrary by the Council for the Protection of Rural England (1992), one of the main results of the British Town and Country Planning system since 1947 "is that the amount of land converted from rural to urban use has been minimized and compacted: urban growth has been contained" (Hall et al. 1973: 393). This was one of the principal policy objectives of the new planning system. It aimed to contain the growth of the major conurbations and large cities and to establish self-contained new towns to accommodate future urban growth.

The inter-war period, especially the 1930s, had been characterized by rapid increases in unplanned, scattered "ribbon development" around the peripheries of the main cities, supplying housing for the growing middle classes who desired ownership of new homes outside the congested inner cities. This process had been encouraged by rising real incomes, gained in the growing service sector industries in which many of them were employed, increases in the availability of credit and the development of new mass transit systems.

A policy of restricting this peripheral development received support from a range of different elite interests. First, there were the planning and design professionals, many of whom followed the ideals of the garden city movement. They were concerned to prevent the coalescence of urban areas, wanting instead to increase the proximity of urban populations to green space. A second set of interests was concerned, in the period following the war, with the need to support the development of the agricultural sector in order to strengthen its capacity to meet the nation's food needs. The prevention of agricultural land losses was thought to be important in this context. The third and most important set of interests behind the strength of the containment policy was comprised of those elites who already formed the population of the countryside around the cities and who wanted to protect the environmental quality of the areas in which they lived against further development.

The main instruments which, it was argued, should be used to implement such a strategy of urban containment, were Green Belts around the conurbations and largest free-standing cities, in which particularly strict control of development was to be maintained. Other types of "designated" land, such as Areas of Outstanding Natural Beauty (AONBs) and national parks, were also added to Green Belts as areas in which particularly strict control of development was exercised. Continuing population expansion was to be accommodated in new and expanded towns.

This section will examine the effects of these policies in three ways. These are:

(a) The seminal debate between Alice Coleman and Robin Best on the degree of containment exercised by the planning system.

(b) The strength of planning controls in designated land areas.

(c) The evaluation of housing provision in old and new locations.

The Coleman versus Best debate

Alice Coleman (1977) argues that the evidence she had gathered showed that 30 years of the town and country planning system had made little impact on the process of scattered development around the periphery of urban areas. The data in Table 6.1 are based on her Second Land Utilization Survey of 1963. They show an increase since 1963 of approximately 50 per cent of the total amount of land in England and Wales under settlement. This represents an increase of 4 per cent in the proportion of the total land area settled. These figures are then extrapolated to present a prediction of the loss of all farmland within 200 to 300 years unless stricter methods of development control are introduced. She highlighted in particular the continuing growth in the area taken up by the "rurban fringe", where the distinction between the built-up area and the countryside is blurred, and which good planning was presumably meant to reduce.

Her conclusions are disputed by Robin Best (1981) & Best and Anderson (1984). Their work is based on painstaking analysis of Ministry of Agriculture statistical returns (Table 6.2). While these data do produce a similar figure to that of Coleman for the total increase in urban land area over the post-war period, the trend in the figures for the average annual transfer of farmland to urban uses points to a reduction from a high point of over 25,000 hectares per annum in the 1930s to a rate of around 15,000 hectares per annum in the period following the introduction of the planning system.

Table 6.2 Transfers of farmland to urban uses: England and Wales, 1920–80.

	Change (ha)	
	Before planning 1920–40	After planning 1945–80
Transfers	80,800	103,300
Annual growth[1]	4,040	2,951

Source: Adapted from Best & Anderson (1984).
Note: 1. Annual growth = the net amount of land transferred from rural to urban uses.

Table 6.2 shows that the average annual conversion of rural to urban land-uses dropped from 4,040 hectares before the introduction of the 1947 policies for urban containment to 2,951 hectares in the 35 years after their introduction. On this basis it is argued that the objective of urban containment has been achieved to quite a large extent. It should be noted, however, that part of the fall in the rate of agricultural land loss in the 1970s and the drop in the urban development rate was caused partly by the stabilization of population growth and the onset of economic recession and high interest rates.

One of the problems with the Coleman and Best debate is that their work is not directly comparable. This problem may be overcome in the future with the use of a standard definition of "urban" areas by the Office of Population Censuses and Surveys (OPCS) combined with the Department of the Environment's Land Use Change Statistics (LUCS). These two sources of data have been brought together by Bibby & Sheperd (1990) to predict *Rates of urbanization in England 1981–2001*. Table 6.3 gives their forecasts of urbanization and urban growth for England up to 2001. Both show low rates of change during the 20-year period. Although they are not directly comparable with the work of Coleman and Best for England and Wales, they show lower rates of increase in urban areas and the conversion of rural to urban land than were discovered by Best & Anderson (1984) for the post-war period. These findings illustrate the fact that commentators expect strict containment policies to continue in Britain.

Table 6.3 Forecasts of land-use changes: England, 1981–2001.

Category of use	1981	2001	Change	Urbanization[1]	Urban growth[2]
	millions of hectares			%	%
Urban	1.3	1.4			
Rural	11.7	11.6	0.1	7.93	0.81
Total	13.0	13.0			

Source: Adapted from Bibby & Sheperd (1990).
Notes: 1. Urbanization = area becoming urban as a % of land in urban use in 1981.
2. Urban growth = area becoming urban as a % of total land in 1981.

Designated land

One of the strongest planning instruments to restrict the conversion of rural to urban land-uses is land designation. This includes the statutory designation of land as:

(a) Green Belt, e.g. the London Green Belt (LGB);
(b) Area of Outstanding Natural Beauty (AONB), e.g. the Chiltern Hills;
(c) National parks, e.g. the Peak District.

Figure 6.1 shows the areas of designated land in Britain.

Figure 6.1 Green belts and other areas of major land-use constraint.

The strength of such strict planning control is demonstrated by Elson (1986). He shows that in the London Green Belt the amount of land taken up by villages and other surface development increased by as little as just over 1,000 hectares between 1963 and 1974. During that period there was only a 1.6 per cent drop in the amount of agricultural land and woodland.

These results are backed up by Wood (1982). Table 6.4 gives an analysis of planning decisions in the High Wycombe area between 1974 and 1981. It highlights the extent of Green Belt control by comparing the rate of refusals of planning permission according to whether the development site is situated on designated Green Belt land or not. Table 6.4 shows that applications for development in designated AONB land were met with a 100 per cent rate of refusal. Green Belt refusals varied between 85 per cent in Green Belt to 93 per cent in land designated as both Green Belt and AONB.

Table 6.4 Planning decisions for residential development by policy notation: High Wycombe area, 1974–81.

Policy notation	Dwellings		
	Permitted	Refused	Refused (%)
London Green Belt			
(LGB)	48	265	85
LGB/AONB	4	54	93
AONB/White Land	0	163	100
White Land	724	764	51
Residential	1,019	665	39
Other	194	56	22
TOTAL	1,989	1,967	50

Source: Adapted from Wood (1982) in Elson (1986).

The work by Bibby & Sheperd (1990), which forms part of the DoE's planning research programme, also confirms the importance of special designations in containing the rate of urban growth. Table 6.5 gives the proportion of land with special designation in each of the regions of England. It also shows the predicted rates of urban growth in each region from 1981 to 2001. The regions are ranked and listed in order of the highest to lowest proportion of specially designated land in 1981. This ranking is then compared with their ranking in terms of highest to lowest predicted rates of urban growth. Their designated land ranking is deducted from their predicted growth ranking. The resulting crude indicator shows that the regions with the highest proportions of designated land tend to have the lowest predicted urban growth rates. Conversely, the regions with the highest predicted growth rates tend to have the lowest proportions of designated land.

The notable exception to the above rule is the South East region. It has both the second highest level of designated land and the highest predicted urban growth rate. Among other things, this shows the significance of economic growth as an explanation of urban growth with or without planning. The South East is now the main engine of the British economy. Strong planning restrictions combined with economic recovery are likely to lead to increasing conflicts in the region over land-uses and planning.

Table 6.5 Designated land and urban growth. Regional rankings: England, 1981–2001.

Region	Designated land 1981 (%) (1)	Urban growth 1981–2001 (2)	Ranking difference (2−1)
North west	45.19	0.72	−5
North	41.30	0.20	−6
South east	40.35	1.27	2
Yorkshire & Humberside	37.65	0.47	−3
South west	37.07	0.83	1
West Midlands	31.47	0.89	4
East Midlands	14.02	0.87	4
East Anglia	10.21	0.83	4

Source: Adapted from Bibby & Sheperd (1990).

Housing

There is no doubt that one of the main effects of the British planning system has been urban containment. But, when one comes to consider in more detail the pattern of new development that did take place, the evidence points to rather less success in meeting the original objective that new urban growth would be directed largely towards balanced self-contained communities in the new and expanded towns. Hall et al. (1973) show that of the new dwellings built in the South East region between 1945 and 1970, only 7.2 per cent were contained in the planned

(1973) show that of the new dwellings built in the South East region between 1945 and 1970, only 7.2 per cent were contained in the planned new and expanded towns, with this proportion falling to just under 4 per cent with respect to England and Wales as a whole (Table 6.6).

Apart from unexpected demographic changes including a more rapid rate of population increase than planners were led to believe, one of the main reasons for this lack of public authority housing is that although it was originally conceived that the majority of new development would be undertaken in the public sector, in fact, from the late 1950s onwards the majority of new housing was being provided privately for owner-occupation (Fig. 6.2).

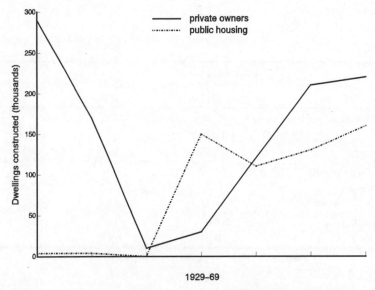

Figure 6.2 Dwellings constructed in England and Wales, 1929–69.

Table 6.6 New towns and expanding towns: contribution to the total housing programme, 1956–70.

Areas	Dwellings (millions)		
	Total completed	In new and expanding towns	
South East	2.2	0.20	7.5%
Rest of England and Wales	4.3	0.08	2.0%
Total	6.5	0.28	3.9%

Source: Adapted from *Housing Statistics, Great Britain,* No. 20, February 1971; *Town and Country Planning,* January 1971. In Hall et al. (1973).

After the 1947 Town and Country Planning Act, the pre-war pattern of scattered speculative housing development was largely restricted, and new private development was located either in higher density housing within the outer parts of the built-up area of the conurbations and free-standing cities or concentrated by planners in substantial pockets of new, relatively high-density development on the less attractive sites in small towns and villages in rural areas beyond the Green Belts. Recent work by Mitchell (1990) points to the fact that, although many commentators have asserted that planning control has been weakened under the Conservative governments of the 1980s, the policies of urban containment have been implemented with even greater force in recent years in the South East as the populations of the counties have sought to protect the local environment from further intrusion.

Suburbanization

Introduction

The second main effect of the British planning system is suburbanization. This "was hardly intended, but arose mainly from attempts to cope willy-nilly with the unexpected and unwelcome population growth, coupled with the lack of really effective local planning powers over the location of employment; it is the growing separation of residential areas from the main centres of employment and other urban facilities or services. . . .[It is] the reverse of what the ideal 1947 system was trying to achieve" (Hall et al. 1973: 393–4).

This definition of suburbanization does not mean simply the growth of suburbs. It is primarily concerned with the locational arrangements of homes and work. It is also concerned with the time and distance between them. This special definition of suburbanization will be examined here by looking at:

(a) changes in the locations of resident populations and employment;
(b) commuting between them.

Population and employment decentralization

Hall et al. (1973) argue that, despite the planned containment of urban growth after the Second World War, market-led decentralization of population occurred in terms of residential location. At the same time, changes in the location of employment did not quite follow the same pattern. They argue that while there did occur relative decentralization of employment from the inner cities of the conurbations and other large cities, this did not occur at such a rapid rate as the decentralization of population. The pattern of employment dispersal was characterized by a process of "re-centralization" in the smaller cities and towns with the consequent growing separation between home and workplace.

During the 1970s and 1980s these changes continued in modified form. The main elements of urban change in Britain during these two decades were:

1 A decline in population and employment in the largest cities, and a tendency for population and employment growth to be concentrated in free-standing cities, and in the small and medium-sized towns located in rural and semi-rural areas;

2 A bias towards growth in the southern part of the country and decline in the north (independently of city-size effects); . . .

3 A tendency for growth to be concentrated in suburban and peri-urban areas, and decline to be concentrated in the inner city (Fielding & Halford 1990: 6).

Champion et al. (1987) used an index composed of data on unemployment rates in 1985, employment change 1971–8 and 1978–81, population change 1971–81, and households with two or more cars in 1981 to rank all of Britain's local labour market areas. The information gained from this exercise provided details of the relative changes taking place in British cities during the 1970s and early 1980s. They were able to show that:

(a) There is a clear north/south divide in Britain. Both levels of prosperity and dynamism are higher in the south than in the north. There is also evidence that this division has become greater in the recent period, partly because of the marked improvement in the position of London in the early to mid 1980s.

116

(b) There is a major arc of prosperity around and to the west of London. Towns such as Horsham, Bracknell, Maidenhead, Basingstoke, High Wycombe, Aldershot and Farnborough are all centres of this prosperity. They are also at or beyond the London Green Belt and are therefore potential generators of additional commuting of the types outlined below.

(c) Only a very few places north and west of the Severn/Wash line have shown both prosperity and growth.

(d) All of the main cities of northern and western Britain perform below the median on both static and change indices.

(e) The prosperous places are doing even better and the areas lacking in prosperity are doing even worse. (Fielding & Halford 1990: 6).

The redistribution of population that accompanied these changes, particularly during the 1970s, can be summed up as "counter-urbanization". Counter-urbanization, or "decentralized urbanization" is indicated by an inverse relationship between net migration rate and settlement size. This means that the larger the city the greater the net migration and loss, and the smaller the town the greater the gain.

The effects of these changes on small and medium sized towns (SAMS) during the 1970s was carried out by Halcrow Fox and Birkbeck College for the DoE (Halcrow Fox 1986). They showed that for SAMS of between 5,000 and 100,000 population, between 1971 and 1981, their populations increased by nearly 6 per cent. During the same period the total population of England grew by less than 1 per cent.

Furthermore, SAMS in the south grew faster than those in the north. Smaller SAMS grew faster than larger ones. There was also a tendency for free-standing SAMS to grow rapidly whatever their size and in whichever region they were located. This growth was associated with increases in the service classes and car ownership. Not too surprisingly, the highest population growth rates were to be found in commuter areas, and also in free-standing and new manufacturing towns (Fielding & Halford 1990: 7).

Among the effects of these changes in population growth rates and their location was the continuation of the trend to separate homes from work. The results of these changes on commuting patterns are described below.

117

The journey to work

A study by the Cambridge Economic Policy Review (1982) examined the changes taking place in commuting patterns for four different types of area between 1951 and 1976. The types of area were:

(a) inner cities;

(b) outer cities;

(c) free-standing cities;

(e) small towns and rural areas.

The results of this analysis are shown in Tables 6.7 – 10.

Table 6.7 gives the relationships between resident population, employment and commuting for Britain's inner cities. It demonstrates that both population of working age and employment declined between 1951 and 1976. Further, it shows, however, that net inward commuting increased. It also shows that an increasing proportion of employment was taken by commuters and a decreasing proportion by local residents. Other things being equal, this led to increasing unemployment among inner-city residents.

In contrast, Table 6.8 shows the same relationships for outer cities during the same period. There population was continuing to decentralize and decline. Employment, on the other hand, was growing. Commuters often went elsewhere for employment. At the time, this left an approximate balance between the numbers of working age and the numbers of jobs. This balance has probably declined since the 1970s with continuing decentralization and economic decline.

Table 6.7 Population, employment and commuting in inner cities: Britain, 1951–76.

	1951 Base 000s	Indices	
		1951 = 100	1976
Population of working age	4,982	100	72
Employment	4,826	100	79
Net inward commuting	997	100	128
Employment minus net commuting	3,829	100	67

Source: Adapted from Cambridge Economic Policy Review (1982).

Table 6.8 Population, employment and commuting in outer cities: Britain, 1951–76.

	1951 base 000s	Indices	
		1951 = 100	1976
Population of working age	6,511	100	68
Employment	3,597	100	108
Net inward commuting	−765	100	71
Employment minus net commuting	4,362	100	101

Source: Adapted from Cambridge Economic Policy Review (1982).

Table 6.9 illustrate some of the re-centralization taking place beyond the metropolitan Green Belts. While population declined slightly in the free-standing cities there, employment increased. This, however, led to even greater proportional increases in inward commuting than in the metropolitan inner cities. The overall result was more commuting but adequate employment in addition to that for the resident workforce.

Table 6.9 Population, employment and commuting in free-standing cities: Britain, 1951–76.

	1951 base 000s	Indices	
		1951 = 100	1976
Population of working age	3,198	100	98
Employment	2,536	100	109
Net inward commuting	189	100	224
Employment minus net commuting	2,347	100	100

Source: Adapted from Cambridge Economic Policy Review (1982).

Table 6.10 Population, employment and commuting in small towns and rural areas: Britain, 1951–76.

	1951 base 000s	Indices	
		1951 = 100	1976
Population of working age	16,555	100	120
Employment	11,176	100	122
Net inward commuting	−421	100	274
Employment minus net commuting	11,597	100	128

Source: Adapted from Cambridge Economic Policy Review (1982).

Table 6.10 shows the level of decentralization of population and employment, for those who could afford it, partly resulting from urban containment. It shows proportionately that the highest levels of population and employment growth were taking place in small towns and rural areas. These were features over which physical land-use planning had little or no control. The move to small towns and rural areas was also accompanied by the largest proportionate increase in commuting to elsewhere.

Taken together Tables 6.7 to 6.10 show the large movements of urban populations and employment that were taking place irrespective of urban containment policies. They also show, however, that in all cases apart from the outer suburbs inward or outward commuting increased. Local planning authorities can be said to have encouraged this process by the zoning of city-centre areas for the traditional commercial uses, while it was the types of people being employed in the service sector industries that located there who were moving out of the city to live. Thus the introduction of the planning system was not able to prevent increasing suburbanization in living patterns.

The time and cost of this added commuting is one of the highest prices paid for the adoption of strict policies of urban containment. This is especially the case when those policies are enforced by the policy instrument of Green Belts. These simply surround cities with a ring, which in many places is not particularly green, and thereby force both employment and people to move otherwise unnecessary distances apart.

Land and housing prices

Introduction

In their analysis of the effects of the British land-use planning system up to the 1970s, Hall et al. (1973) showed that the increase between the price of land "ripe for residential development" in the late 1930s and that with planning permission in the late 1960s was between ten and twenty-fold. They go on to say that "As a result, the proportion of land cost in the total final housing cost has risen from between 4 and 12 per cent, in 1960, to between 18 and 38 per cent, by 1970" (Hall et al. 1973: 399–400). They argue that these increases were not the result of rising demand for housing. Demand for housing actually decreased during the latter half of the 1960s. They were essentially the result of the constraints placed upon housing land supply, in the places where households wanted to live, by their local planning authorities.

While developers started to compensate for rises in housing land prices by using smaller sites, the planners preferred to deal with large, comprehensively developed sites. The scale of these preferred operations favoured the large-scale builders who could afford to purchase the larger sites and develop them over longer periods of time.

Developers also adjusted to rising land prices by building at greater densities on smaller plots. At the "cheaper" end of the market this meant that "For many owner-occupiers the standard of housing was lower than that set down by the Parker Morris standards for rented local authority housing" (Hall et al. 1973: 401). Much of this housing permitted by the planning system was of poor architectural design. It contained inadequate space standards for a consumer society looking to emulate the equipment and facilities seen in the kinds of Californian houses so often portrayed on film, television and in advertisements.

The county planning authorities preferred to accommodate the "expensive" end of the housing market. Rather than allowing urban growth around their larger towns and cities, "they wished to maintain the existing character of the area and therefore the limited land release that was allowed permitted low-density, high value development near villages and small towns" (Hall et al. 1973: 401).

The net effects of these planning policies were to trade off space standards and the quality of housing for some groups against the containment of urban growth and the preservation of private open space mostly for other groups. The outcome has been that the operation of the planning system has distributed various costs and benefits between different social groups. This is the inevitable result of the different location and costs of different land-uses described in this section combined with the extension of residential and social segregation described below.

This section will be divided into three parts. These will follow the development of the debate on land and house prices initiated by Hall et al. (1973). The parts are:

(a) Evans versus Grigson;
(b) Cheshire & Sheppard;
(c) Eve and the Department of Land Economy, Cambridge.

The first part analyzes the debate between Alan Evans and William Grigson on whether land-use planning has had any effects on land prices. The second part looks at the Paul Cheshire and John Sheppard comparison of the planning regimes of Reading and Darlington and their effects on housing prices and standards. The third part discusses the most comprehensive study of these issues, the DoE study of *The relationship between house prices and land supply* (1992), conducted by Gerald Eve Surveyors and the Department of Land Economy at Cambridge.

Evans versus Grigson

There has been a contention that the government's land policies, including the planning system, have not only failed to control land values, but indeed have contributed to their rapid increases. Evans (1988) uses data from the Department of the Environment's index of housing land prices to show that land values rose some 1,000 per cent between 1969 and 1985 against a 400 per cent increase in the general retail price index. He concluded that the containment policies of the planning system have, indeed, restricted the overall supply of land for new housing development and thus placed added pressure on the land market so that land values have risen rapidly, and this in turn has forced up house prices.

Grigson (1986), however, in a report commissioned by the London and South East Regional Planning Conference (SERPLAN), argued that the South East region had been pulling its weight in new house building and that the rise in house prices had not been exceptional. He emphasized that the ratio of house prices to incomes in the South East had remained level over time. The prices of both South East land and housing relative to the national level had remained steady.

Nevertheless, his analysis only examines the ratios after the introduction of the London Green Belt. He is, therefore, not comparing the situation before and after the introduction of strict planning controls. Furthermore, while the ratios for London itself have been falling, possibly due to the exodus of people and jobs, those for the Rest of the South East (ROSE) (where Table 6.5 shows one of the highest regional proportions of designated land in England), have remained above the national average. In recent years they have begun to increase even further above that average (Grigson 1986).

Evans (1988) is therefore clearly right to draw attention to the disproportionate rise in housing land prices. They have been higher than those of the retail price index and much higher than the price of agricultural land which has been preserved from development by local land-use plans.

Cheshire & Sheppard

Cheshire & Sheppard (1989) collected and compared data on house prices in Reading and Darlington as examples of areas subject to different planning regimes in terms of restrictiveness in releasing land for housing development. Reading was used as an example of a restrictive planning regime in the south east of England; Darlington was used as an example of a relaxed regime in the north.

They showed that although households in Reading, particularly those lower in the income scale, tended to be better off than those in Darlington, their houses were, relative to their incomes, more expensive. Furthermore, by applying the data to a model of the housing market based on conventional neo-classical urban economic theory, including adjustments for household incomes, size of community and transport costs, they made estimations of the effect on house prices in Reading of a relaxation of planning policy to allow more market-led development.

123

The results of this analysis are shown in Table 6.11.

Table 6.11 Estimated house prices in Reading under alternative planning regimes. 1984 prices; constant plot sizes.

House type	Regime			
	Reading existing		Reading as Darlington	
	Distance from centre (ft)			
	4,000	18,000	4,000	18,000
Flats				
Price (£)	26,758	25,361	25,669	24,947
% change			−4.2	−1.7
Detached				
Price (£)	77,066	65,123	68,870	62,664
% change			−11.9	−3.9

Source: Adapted from Cheshire & Sheppard (1989: 469–85).

Table 6.11 shows that if Reading adopted the same relaxed planning regime as Darlington, flats near the centre would be around 4 per cent cheaper and those further out would be about 2 per cent cheaper. The greatest difference, however, would be for the type of houses using the most land. In Britain these are detached houses. This type of house would be nearly 12 per cent cheaper near the centre of Reading and nearly 4 per cent cheaper further out if the planning regime there was as relaxed as that in Darlington.

Cheshire & Sheppard (1989) also estimated how access to different types of housing is affected by the planning regime in terms of the income level needed to obtain a mortgage for the necessary amount. While first-time buyers would be able to buy the cheapest possible housing with an income of £232 a year less under a relaxation of planning control in Reading, for the household moving to a 3-bedroom semi the move could have been made on an income of £912 a year less, and to a 4-bedroom detached house for £2,422 less. They argue that this suggests that the system of restrictive planning controls financially restricts upward movement in the housing market considerably more than it restricts the ability to purchase any house.

They then adapted the analysis to account for the fact that if planning policies were relaxed and land prices fell, people would tend to consume more land. In this case, the model predicts an increase in average plot sizes of 65 per cent – with a corresponding increase in the entire urban area of Reading of approximately 50 per cent – with the effect that the extent of the drop in house prices is reduced slightly from that shown in Table 6.11. This part of the analysis thus indicates the impact of planning restraint on the economic welfare of households in terms of their lower consumption of living space, in addition to the increased prices they have to pay.

Eve and the Department of Land Economy, Cambridge

The Department of the Environment commissioned Gerald Eve, Surveyors and the Department of Land Economy, Cambridge, as part of its Planning Research Programme, to conduct a study, *The relationship between house prices and land supply* (1992). This is the most authoritative study of these effects of the land-use planning system to date.

Again, the study used the comparative method. This time two towns in the south east of England were compared with two in the north. They ranged from Reigate and Banstead in Surrey through Wokingham in Berkshire to Beverley in Humberside and Barnsley in South Yorkshire. Reigate had the most consistently tough and contained housing land release policies over the period of study, which was 1969 to 1989. Barnsley had the least restrictive planning regime and was therefore used as the yardstick by which to compare the effects of the others.

The study had four objectives. These were to:

1 Clarify the relationship in the short, medium and long terms between house prices and land supply.
2 Assess the means by, and extent to which, planning policies influence land supply.
3 Assess the extent to which the response in terms of the amount of new buildings and the prices charged, is influenced by land supply.
4 Assess what effect changes in land supply would have on the level, rate and rise of house prices (Eve & Department of Land Economy 1992: 47).

The consultants define the short run as a period of less than 2 years, the medium term as 2–5 years and the longer term as over 5 years. In the short term the supply of housing is relatively fixed. This is because the case studies showed that it takes about 2 years from the submission of a planning application to the completion of new housing units. This limitation combined with a restricted flow of building land means that, in Britain, sudden large increases in demand generate price increases. There have been three major property booms in Britain since the Second World War that illustrate this phenomenon. These took place between 1971 and 1973, 1978 and 1980, and 1985 and 1989. They are shown in Table 6.12.

Table 6.12 Housing land prices and prices of new houses after accounting for inflation: England and Wales, 1968–88.

Year	"Real" land price per plot	"Real" price of new houses
	Base year 1985 = 100	
1968	49	72
1969	57	75
1970	55	75
1971	58	75
1972	91	88
1973	129	109
1974	110	108
1975	61	92
1976	53	87
1977	48	81
1978	54	87
1979	67	95
1980	75	99
1981	70	95
1982	72	91
1983	78	95
1984	84	96
1985	100	100
1986	123	112
1987	153	124
1988	223	148

Source: Adapted from Holmans (1990).

Table 6.12 shows that, after allowing for inflation, real land plot prices increased by 350 per cent between 1968 and 1988. Over the same period house prices increased by 104 per cent. "Thus housing land prices rose at more than double the rate of increase in house prices. Furthermore, the land price data are in terms of plots which tended to reduce in size so the price per unit of land has increased even faster" (Eve & Department of Land Economy 1992: 23).

In the medium and long term the supply of land is not fixed. It is influenced by the way in which local planning authorities adjust their plans, the emergence of "windfall" sites not previously identified by LPAs and the general economic and political climate. Nevertheless, the planning system does operate constraints over the supply of land. The effects of these constraints can be seen in the differences between housing and agricultural land prices in the four case study areas. These are shown in Table 6.13.

Table 6.13 Housing land and agricultural land prices in the case study areas, 1975–90.

	Land type		
	Housing (£ per ha)	Agriculture (£ per ha)	Agricultural land price as % of housing land price
Reigate			
1975	75,000	1,630	2.2
1990	972,000	4,940	0.5
Wokingham			
1975	67,000	1,980	3.0
1990	1,070,000	6,790	0.6
Beverley			
1975	19,000	1,750	9.2
1990	480,000	4,940	1.0
Barnsley			
1975	27,000	1,450	5.4
1990	210,000	6,180	2.9

Source: Adapted from Eve & Department of Land Economy (1992: 26, Table 7).

Table 6.13 shows that planning constraints on the supply of land are significant not just in the South East but also in the North. In 1975 housing land prices were 46 times agricultural land prices in Reigate and 19 times those in Barnsley. By 1990 they were 197 times those in

Reigate and 34 times those even in Barnsley. "Thus, all the evidence points to the planning system having a significant effect on land supply. The outcomes of this constraint include higher land prices, and less land coming forward for development" (Eve & Department of Land Economy 1992: 49).

The constraints imposed on land supply by LPAs influence both the form of new housing and its price. In the first place, densities have been increased and average plot sizes reduced. In the second place, the price of these smaller and denser houses has also been increased.

Table 6.14 shows the changes taking place in housing density in the case study areas between 1950 and 1980. In all cases where data were available it demonstrates generally increasing densities. By the late 1980s the average density of 3 or 4 bedroom detached houses in Reigate was 29.2 per hectare. The density was even higher in Barnsley, but that was the result of a one-off unique circumstance.

Table 6.14 Density of 3–4 bed detached housing per hectare in the case study areas, 1950–80.

Towns	Density per hectare				
	1950s	1960s	1970s	Early 1980s	Late 1980s
Reigate	20.14	9.75	18.16	23.86	29.92
Wokingham	16.72	15.65	25.55	23.11	21.77
Beverley	na	14.38	22.09	na	27.38
Barnsley	na	39.44	27.11	40.94	na

Source: Adapted from Eve & Department of Land Economy (1992: 31, Table 8).

The relationships between house prices and density are also shown by changes in the types of new houses built in the UK since the Second World War. Table 6.15 gives the prices of different types of house built in the UK between 1969 and 1989. It shows that price increases have been greatest for those houses using the most land. Thus increases in the price of terraced houses have averaged just over 1,000 per cent. Increases on detached houses have averaged nearly 1,500 per cent.

The consultants go on to analyze the effects on house prices resulting from planning constraints on land supply in the case study areas. They do this by calculating the difference between the cost of the land element in housing and the "opportunity cost" of that land.

Table 6.15 House prices (£ sterling) by house types, UK 1969–89.

	Terrace	House types Semi-detached	Detached	Bungalow
1969	3,605	4,217	6,722	4,619
1989	42,249	52,022	105,861	66,812
Increase (%)	1,072%	1,134	1,475	1,346

Source: Adapted from Eve & Department of Land Economy (1992: 40, Table 11).

Opportunity cost is an economist's term meaning the opportunities given up or foregone by doing one thing rather than others. In the case of housing land in the case study areas, the opportunity cost of that land is defined as the housing land prices in Barnsley. This is because they were sufficient to induce the transfer of land from other uses, or opportunities, to residential uses in conditions where the land supply is least constrained by planning.

Table 6.16 gives the results of these calculations; the key column is the right hand one. It "gives an estimate of the possible reduction that could be secured in house prices if the constraint on land supply were relaxed and all additional land supply could be made available at the assumed opportunity cost" (Eve & Department of Land Economy 1992: 45).

Table 6.16 The effect of constrained land supply on house prices: Reigate, Wokingham and Beverley, 1975–90.

	(1) House price	(2) Plot value	(3) Opportunity land cost	(4) Difference (2 − 3)	(5) % of house price (4 ÷ 1)
Reigate					
1975	23,000	6,700	2,450	4,250	18
1990	140,000	69,000	18,850	50,150	36
Wokingham					
1975	18,500	3,750	1,550	2,200	12
1990	115,000	60,650	11,900	48,750	42
Beverley					
1975	17,500	1,150	1,650	−500	−3
1990	100,000	29,200	12,800	16,400	16

Source: Adapted from Eve & Department of Land Economy (1992: 45, Table 14).
Note: Barnsley plot values are used as the Opportunity Land Cost in Col. 3.

It may be seen that land supply constraints, mostly as a result of land-use planning regimes, have pushed up the price of housing by 36 per cent in Reigate, 42 per cent in Wokingham and even by 16 per cent in Beverley. Not only had planning increased the price of new housing by these amounts by 1990, but also the degree of increase had itself accelerated since 1975. This indicates that continuing constraints operating in the places where most people want to live – partly because of the availability of employment there – are likely to contribute to further house price rises after the current slump in both the economy and house prices comes to an end.

The result of these different factors is that developers are now producing more smaller dwellings than ever before. This is the opposite of what would be expected with rising affluence. In such circumstances it would be expected that consumers would demand larger and better quality housing. There is some evidence of this in the increasing size of housing in California shown above. In Britain, however, the consultants found that developers have not constructed better quality housing in any of the case study areas except in Beverley during the 1980s. Instead, there has been a shift away from the construction of bungalows and detached houses on larger plots to the development of flats and terraced houses at higher densities on smaller plots of land.

The local planning system has responded to some of these problems during the 1980s at the insistence of the central government and DoE. LPAs now have to cooperate with the House Builders' Federation (HBF), which represents the large volume builders, to ensure that structure plans contain adequate and realistic 5-year supplies of housing land. This has resulted in the identification of more and larger plots, particularly in the South East (Simmie 1986). The processing of planning applications has been speeded up. However, none of these measures has had much impact on land and housing prices.

The consultants conclude that "it would require significant additional land release on a national scale, and over a considerable time period, to have a measurable effect on house prices" (Eve & Department of Land Economy 1992). This is far in excess of anything proposed by the current constraint policies of the British land-use planning system.

The effects of planning on economic growth

Introduction

In addition to the very significant increases in land and housing prices analyzed above, there are two groups of effects that land-use planning has on economic growth. The first group are effects that arise as a consequence of the uses of land and buildings whose location and type have been determined by the planning system. These are indirect effects of the planning system itself. The second group arises as a direct result of the costs and benefits which the planning system imposes on land-uses and development. These are direct costs that may help or hinder the immediate elements of economic growth which arise directly as a result of planning decisions.

The indirect effects of planning on economic growth are almost impossible to measure. Hall et al. (1973) came to the conclusion that these are effects "of the planning system, on which it is impossible to be certain . . . in the nature of the phenomenon it is impossible to arrive at a quantified estimate of the effect" (Hall et al. 1973: 405). Although many of the planners whom they interviewed in the course of their study thought that it was "probable" that the planning system had reduced the rate of economic growth, they were not able to produce any evidence one way or the other.

Despite this continuing lack of evidence on the indirect effects of the planning system on economic growth, Michael Heseltine accused it of keeping "Jobs locked in filing cabinets" in 1978 while he was the Shadow Minister for the Environment. This set the tone of the incoming Conservative government's attitude to planning during the 1980s. The Department of Trade and Industry (DTI) produced a report called *Burdens on business* (1985). This was followed by a White Paper called *Lifting the burden* (1985) produced by the DoE. In so far as they were concerned with land-use planning, they were critical of the ability of plans to keep up with contemporary trends. It was assumed that the best indicator of these trends is the market. Therefore the government has been reshaping the purpose of planning in order to aid the market.

Despite such government efforts, the difficulties of producing empirical evidence on the indirect effects of land-use planning on economic growth have not been overcome so far. They cannot, therefore, be discussed as anything much more than a matter of opinion. For these reasons the discussion cannot be taken any further at this point.

The rest of this section will therefore be devoted to an analysis of the direct costs and benefits of the land-use planning system. An assessment will be made of their immediate effects on economic growth directly connected with the development.

The direct costs and benefits of the land-use planning system can be divided into three main categories. These are:

(a) cash costs such as taxes on betterment and charges on applications for permission to develop;

(b) financial costs arising from planning agreements or delays imposed by the operation of development control;

(c) benefits of the planning system.

These three categories will form the basis of the organization of this section.

Cash payments to public authorities

The most immediate cash cost of the planning system was the abortive attempts to tax the difference in price between land without and land with planning permission. There have been three ultimately unsuccessful Labour government attempts to do this.

The first attempt, in 1947, subjected any increases in land prices arising from the granting of planning permission to a 100 per cent development charge. The effects of this charge either removed any incentive to develop so reducing economic growth; or encouraged developers to pass on the development charge to consumers. This was inflationary and therefore also tended to reduce economic growth by reducing the amount of investment available for other economic uses. This provision of the 1947 act was abolished by the Conservatives in the Town and Country Planning Act 1953. There was a return to a free market in land.

The result of the free market, together with some planning control, was that private development became increasingly speculative. Site values were increased by up to ten times their existing use values and public authorities were increasingly unable to compete for land at such inflated prices. These inflationary pressures also helped to limit the amount of investment available for other uses.

A second attempt to acquire betterment by public authorities was made by the Labour government in 1967 in the form of the Land Commission Act. This legislation was intended to ensure that land was available for the implementation of national, regional and local plans, as well as to recoup some of the development value for the community. Development land would be purchased by the commission at current market value and sold at the best possible price. Land for essential development would, however, be sold below market price. A development charge was set at 40 per cent payable when the development value was realized. Here the government believed that the scheme would still provide an incentive to sell land in response to demand.

However, within three years the Conservative government had repealed the Land Commission legislation. At the act's demise, the commission had purchased only 2,800 acres and sold 400 acres. The commission was also seen as inflationary because sellers both withheld land from the market in order to avoid incurring the levy in anticipation of it being repealed in the near future, and thereby restricting supply (Balchin & Bull 1987); and also paid the levy to the buyers but then added at least part of it to the price which they charged the very same buyers (Hall et al. 1973).

The last Labour attempt to acquire betterment was the Community Land Act 1975. This time the local authorities were to take over development land and to keep some of the remaining profit, sharing the remainder with other local authorities and the Treasury. In practice, though, the result was much the same as previous attempts in having only a marginal effect on land purchases and sales. Predictably the act was repealed in 1980 by the Conservatives. Development Land Tax was retained until 1985, when a free market in land was again restored.

None of these attempts to tax betterment actually worked for any length of time or as intended. In so far as they had any direct effects on economic growth they probably retarded it. This is because their main effects were always to reduce the supply and raise the price of building land. In so far as development therefore required more investment than would otherwise have been the case, investment and growth in other economic activities could have been retarded.

A more recent direct cash cost of planning was introduced in 1981. It is the practice of charging fees for making planning applications. These are now payable for most types of application. They range from £55 for a domestic extension to £5,520 for the largest building application. They were originally intended to cover half the costs of processing applications. Eventually, however, it is intended that they will cover the entire costs of development control (Audit Commission 1992: 20).

About 82 per cent of planning applications are now fee earning (Audit Commission 1992: 5). But the limitation of £5,520 for the largest buildings means that these fees are an insignificant proportion of the total cost of the most important types of development. Conversely, the fees charged for the smallest house extensions are probably subsidizing those of the largest applications.

At the moment the levels of fees charged for making planning applications are not so great as to have much impact on development proposals. They are therefore unlikely to reduce economic growth contingent upon the flow of construction projects.

Costs for developers

The second group of planning actions that may affect economic growth are those that increase costs for developers. These include planning agreements and delays.

British planning agreements are not the same as those made between developers and the planning system in California. In Britain the local planning authorities have the power to enter into legal agreements with developers which may impose on the developer "an obligation to carry out works not included in the development for which permission has been sought or to make some payment to confer some extraneous right in return for permitting development to take place" (Department of the

Environment 1983). The results are known as "planning gain".

The statutory bases of planning gain are section 52 of the Town and Country Planning Act 1971, now superseded by section 106 of the Town and Country Planning Act 1990; section 126 of the Housing Act 1974 and section 40 of the Highways Act 1959. On the one hand, planning gains may be seen as the communities' share of development gain. On the other hand, they can be seen as attempts to buy planning permission, even to the extent that a planning gain deal may allow an unsatisfactory scheme to go ahead or a satisfactory scheme to fail.

Table 6.17 shows the types and proportions of "gains" acquired through the granting of bargained planning permissions. It may be seen that the potentially more costly of the gains shown form the lower proportions of bargains. Thus the provision of community buildings, rehabilitation of property, provision of infrastructure and the gift of buildings for residential use make up only 6 per cent each of the total bargains struck by local planning authorities in this study.

The scale of planning gains remains relatively modest. It is not known whether the main developments permitted as a result of providing some community gains are significant enough to influence average land or house prices. It is unlikely that the costs of planning agreements have a significant effect on economic growth. This is partly because

Table 6.17 Types and proportions of planning gains.

Type of land use	%
Specification of use	24
Public rights of way to the developer's land	16
Dedication of land to public use	15
Extinguishing existing user rights	14
Provision of community buildings	6
Rehabilitation of property	6
Provision of infrastructure	6
Gift or sale of buildings for residential use	6
Commuted payments for car parking	6
TOTAL $N = 100\%$[1]	104[2]

Source: Adapted from Jowell (1977: 414-33).
Notes:
1. Numbers do not sum to 100 due to consistent rounding.
2. This figure represents the total number of bargains.

local planning authorities can usually only acquire them in circumstances where economic and development growth are already taking place. It is very difficult to negotiate any planning gains in places where economic decline has set in.

The fourth and final direct cost of planning which has been argued to slow economic growth is delay. There is an extensive literature on the effect of land-use planning delays particularly with respect to housing. The Economist Intelligence Unit (1975) and the House Builders' Federation during the 1980s both argued that delays in modifying plans and in making development control decisions added to the costs of developers and therefore contributed to slowing the rate of economic growth. There was not much hard evidence to support these arguments but, after 1979, the Conservative government put a great deal of emphasis on encouraging LPAs to speed up their decision making processes. The government itself also streamlined the appeals procedures.

The DoE set LPAs the target of deciding 80 per cent of planning applications within eight weeks. In the year 1990/1 the LPAs in England decided just over half a million planning applications. This was a little less than the numbers decided in the property boom year of 1988/9 (Audit Commission 1992). Despite central government protestations to the contrary, the proportion of these applications decided within eight weeks had actually fallen from 70 per cent in 1982/3 to 46 per cent in 1989/90. Very few LPAs meet the DoE target of deciding 80 per cent of applications within eight weeks (Audit Commission 1992: 8). On the face of it, this would indicate an increase in costs and possible reductions in rates of economic growth as a direct result of increasing delays to development caused by the planning system.

Developers are very sensitive to planning delays and the costs that they may impose. This is particularly true in boom periods such as 1988/9 when developers were not able to increase completions in order to take advantage of the sellers' market at those times. Nevertheless, over the long term, Eve & Department of Land Economy (1992) found that over the 20 years they studied there had been a reduction in the time taken to move from the submission of a planning application to completion on site. This was most apparent in the case study towns of Wokingham and Beverley where the process took over six years in the early 1970s and had been reduced to three or four years by the late 1980s.

"In general terms it took at least 3 years to increase housing supply in the early 1970s. In 1990 that time period has been reduced to about 2 years" (Eve & Department of Land Economy 1992: 35). These time constraints were partly a result of delays in reaching planning decisions and partly a result of the developers' own organizational limitations. Both contributed to reductions in the rate of development and economic growth.

Benefits of the planning system

There are some counter-arguments to those advanced above. They assert that planning may actually increase economic growth, either by reducing the costs of development or by making more efficient use of physical investments. There are four such arguments. They are that the planning system could reduce the cost of housing by:

(a) maintaining a pipeline of land-use planning permissions and the phasing of development;
(b) providing information;
(c) the better organization of land;
(d) making more efficient use of infrastructure.

The phasing of land release by the planning system could reduce costs by providing a known supply. This is because developers could assess the future price of housing because of the known volume in the pipeline. They could also focus their attention on land likely to attract planning permission rather than waste time on land where permissions will not be given.

Since 1980 the government has encouraged LPAs to conduct joint land availability studies with the volume house-builders. These provide information on the five-year supply of building land.

Planning may be able to improve the organization of sites. This could make more locations viable for developers and so reduce their overall costs.

Finally, planning may encourage both the more efficient use of infrastructure and better quality than would otherwise be provided. "All these factors suggest that it is possible for the planning system to reduce the cost of building to developers, but the evidence . . . suggests that these benefits are not great" (Eve & Department of Land Economy 1992: 34).

In the first place, infrastructure costs are a small proportion of development costs. They are typically less than 10 per cent so there is not much scope for significant cost savings. Secondly, any land constraints tend to increase the price that developers are prepared to bid for it. This leads to inflation. Thirdly, the organization of a pipeline also constrains supply both by excluding development from other sites and by making available some sites which are not yet economically viable. The net effect of these planning actions may therefore be to push up costs, cause inflation and reduce the amount of investment available for other purposes. All these results could contribute to the slowing of development and economic growth in that sector and elsewhere.

Residential and social segregation

Introduction

The ideology of British town planning, particularly among its founding fathers, contains a strong belief in the twin ideas of community and social balance (Simmie 1971). Many plans have contained, as part of their overall objectives, the idea that people do or should want to live in socially balanced communities. What is quite clear from the available evidence, however, is that most people do not want to do any such thing. One thing which is distinctive about Britain is the "tendency to differentiate the 'favoured' from the 'unfavoured' environments, and the consequent tendency to spatial class segregation [which has] developed to such a very marked degree. It is not only particular streets, quarters, or even parts of the cities which are thus socially labelled in Britain, but entire tracts of the national territory, or even regions, which have thus acquired particular predominant class connotations" (Reade 1987: xi).

Such differences at the national scale can be inferred from work by Champion & Green (1988) which "rates places" according to their "local dynamism". Prosperity and dynamism are associated with the residential presence of the higher and service social classes. The researchers found that both were higher in the south than in the north. Secondly, they found that there is a major arc of growth and prosperity around the west of London. Thirdly, there are a few places north and west of the Severn/Wash line that have both prosperity and growth. Fourthly, they found that all the main cities of northern and western Britain perform below the median. Finally, and most importantly from the point of view of the discussion here, the prosperous places are doing even better and the areas lacking in prosperity are doing even worse (Champion & Green 1988). Thus residential location in Britain is crucial in terms of access to life chances.

Not only have the distinctions between places in Britain been changing but so also has the class structure. The main changes in the class structure as a whole have been the rapid growth of the service class composed of professional, technical and managerial workers, a decline in male manual work and an increase in unemployment (Goldthorpe et al. 1987). Members of the service class tend to live in the more prosperous national areas while manual workers and the unemployed are found more often in the less prosperous areas and the inner cities.

Land-use planning is not a major cause of these national trends. Nevertheless, instead of being used to change them and contribute to the creation of socially balanced communities, it has more often been used to preserve class domination and class privilege. According to Reade (1987), the main device for achieving this objective has been "physical exclusion". He argues that

Much of the empirical evidence concerning the *actual* effects of town and country planning in Britain . . . clearly demonstrates the considerable extent to which the planning system has been used as a means of securing spatial class segregation. What this research evidence refers to as the "containment" of the cities is in fact virtually synonymous with . . . the "exclusion" of the less privileged (Reade 1987: xii).

This section examines these issues in three ways. They are:

(a)   social class, family life cycle and ethnic residential segregation;

(b)   housing types and locations;

(c)   access to public goods.

It will be argued that planning has contributed to the residential seg-regation of families from different social classes and at different stages of their life cycles. In general, the advantages conferred by occupying the better housing in better locations have been acquired by higher social classes. Ethnic minorities have fared the worst. Finally, different residential locations provide access to possibilities for the consumption of different public goods and services such as transport, parks, schools and health services. Land-use planning has also contributed to the dis-tribution of these possibilities to better-off rather than worse-off members of local areas.

Social class, family life cycle and ethnic residential segregation

Social class polarization is a feature of British society as a whole. Goldthorpe et al. (1987) have shown that it is now especially associated with the growth of the service class and its marked differentiation from manual workers and the unemployed. These differences are both reflec-ted in and reinforced by the residential segregation of the different social classes.

In their study of British cities, Champion & Green (1988) found evi-dence not only of widening differences between different social groups at the national level, but also signs of a social polarization between north and south, between the industrial city and the urbanized country-side, and between the inner city, the outer council estates and the rest of the urban area. Research on residential segregation within cities gen-erally confirms this picture. It shows that the working class tends to be located in the inner city and in peripheral council estates. The middle classes live in the suburbs. The Afro-Caribbeans and the Asians are con-centrated in the inner cities (Fielding & Halford 1990: 47).

One of the key features of social and urban change has been the differential presence and uneven growth of the service class. One concept used to describe its impact on cities is gentrification. This term was coined by Ruth Glass to denote a process of inner-city neighbourhood social change which results in the replacement of a long-established manual working-class population, often living in privately rented accommodation, by a career-orientated, non-manual middle-class population of owner-occupiers. Research shows that, in prosperous cities, gentrification has transformed some inner-city areas. This is often despite the planners' ideological stance on the maintenance of these traditional communities (Fielding & Halford 1990: xiv).

Important as it has been in some inner-city areas, gentrification has been even more significant in rural areas. Partly as a result of containment policies, gentrification has been an important feature of social and physical change in the countryside (Newby 1979; Pahl 1965). This is particularly true in those areas located within the commuting range of a large city or possessing special landscape qualities (Fielding & Halford 1990: 55). These important changes are closely related to planning policies and the abilities of rural land owners and the service class to influence what those policies are.

In addition to social class residential segregation family life cycle and ethnic spatial separation are also common in Britain. Dale (1987) shows how selective the post-war process of suburbanization has been with respect to stages in the life cycles of families. She shows that couples with children are to be found in the inner-suburbs and in the outer council estates. Older working couples without children tend to live in the outer private estates. The single elderly tend to be divided between the poorer inner city or outside the city altogether.

Ethnic segregation is also common and highly visible in Britain. As in California, black ethnic groups tend to be concentrated in the inner areas of the larger cities. These are often associated with poor quality privately rented housing. Unlike their counterparts in the rural commuter belts, their residents have little influence over planning policies.

This section has been used to establish the nature and extent of social and residential segregation in Britain. This is a particularly important phenomenon for land-use planning. This is because, on the one hand, the ideology of planning has been concerned to produce, by physical means, the opposite of segregation and, on the other hand, the location and types of land-uses and buildings, which make significant changes to particular places, are the major concern of planning. Decisions to use land for certain purposes in one place will affect the social groups that live there. Because different social groups live in different places such planning decisions usually affect different places and groups differently. The next two sections will therefore analyze what contributions planning decisions on land-uses have made to different types of place and consequently to different social classes, families and ethnic groups.

Housing types and locations

During the late 1960s and early 1970s major changes were taking place in the British urban system. Selective groups of people and jobs were moving away from the larger and older cities. This process is known as counter-urbanization or decentralized urbanization. It meant that more of the service class was to be found in the outer suburbs, smaller towns and villages. They were therefore the group most affected by planning policies for those types of area. Usually, planning control in these rural counties has led to a restricted pattern of housing development for owner occupation.

Meanwhile, in the inner cities the city planning authorities were developing programmes of urban renewal in an attempt to improve the living conditions of the urban populations not able to move out. As Dunleavy (1981) has noted, rather than encouraging the ideals of decentralization, the fundamental post-war planning approach to the inner cities was to attempt to deal with the problems of an urban area *in situ*, a solution contained in part in the Forshaw and Abercrombie plan for the County of London (Forshaw & Abercrombie 1943). These plans defined rings of density ranging from some 200 persons per acre (ppa) in the centre, through intermediate areas at 136 ppa and to a suburban zone at 50 ppa. In effect, these designations marked a conservative acceptance of what were essentially market allocations – a process labelled "trend planning" by Dunleavy – rather than providing for some more radical reshaping of land-uses.

Such a planning policy also reflected the wishes of both the city and county authorities. The city authorities wanted to keep the urban populations within their boundaries and thereby, it was hoped, stave off the decline of both their rateable-value base and their electoral support. The county authorities wanted to contain the spread of the cities so that they could not make future claims on their territory and also to keep the *hoi polloi* out of the small towns and villages and so preserve their social status.

In addition, since the planning system was also directed towards providing more open space and improved transport infrastructure (in conditions of urban containment), high-density development was thought to be necessary, particularly in the congested inner areas. Dunleavy also suggests that at the same time as these pressures were coming to bear, architects independently began to argue that high density development, particularly of a high-rise nature, could be made compatible with improvements in amenity. The Forshaw-Abercrombie plan had determined the orthodoxy that densities of over 100 ppa could only be achieved through high-rise building. The result in practice was a major offensive in slum clearance and comprehensive redevelopment in an effort to sanitize working-class living environments (for examples of this, see Paris 1977, on Birmingham; and Mason 1977, on Manchester).

Reviewing the effects of these policies, Hall et al. (1973) have assessed their distributional effects on different groups living in different types of places. They argue that the gainers have been:

(a) The ex-urbanites who use the countryside as a way of life rather than a way of work. For them planning has established a civilized British version of apartheid and preserves their status quo. This group has gained more and lost less than any other. It has been quick to recognize the implications of public participation in planning in order to reinforce its position.

(b) The new suburbanites who have bought homes in the new developments. They have benefited from owner occupation. They have lost in the amount of land and house space that these new developments have provided. As shown above; planning restrictions have driven up the price of land and housing. Developers have cushioned these effects by building more, smaller houses on each acre of land.

(c)   Tenants in public housing have gained. This is particularly if the accommodation was built after 1965 when the Parker-Morris design and space standards were introduced for public authority housing developments. Until recently, such tenants would have lost the advantages of capital appreciation on their property. During the 1980s, however, they have been given the right to buy their council houses, often at a large discount on the full market price.

The losers have been:

(a)   The ruralites who owned land who might have sold it for development had they not been prevented from doing so by being unable to acquire planning permission.

(b)   The less affluent suburbanites without cars. They live in environments where the lack of a car represents an increasing hardship.

(c)   The groups that have had the worst deal have been those poorer city dwellers living in the private rented housing sector. This is heavily concentrated in older property in the metropolitan cores. These groups have been left behind by economic and social change. They have not been able to use the planning system to do much about their lot. The sale of council houses and the rundown of council building programmes offer them no way out of their predicament.

Access to public goods

One of the important effects of planning is to open up or close off access to what economists call pure and impure public goods and services. These are basically goods and services which markets do not provide either because it is difficult to charge for their use, for example light houses, or because most people could not afford them at market prices, for example health, education and social security. Because many of these public goods are located in different places and provided to different standards, access to them tends to differ according to where people live. The land-use arrangement of these relationships is an important part of planning.

Although not directly related to planning *per se*, a study of differences in ill-health and health care by Curtis & Mohan (1989) illustrates the important difference that access to public goods such as health care make to life chances. They showed that there is a growing divide between those who are well served as opposed to those who are poor in their access to health care, and that this is leading to a widening of social class and spatial differences in mortality and morbidity.

With respect to planning, Simmie (1981) studied the effects of planning decisions on areas with different social class compositions over a 21-year period. This study showed that, in Oxford, planning permitted more development relevant to the needs of higher-class residents in their residential areas than to any other groups. Conversely, it permitted development to become less appropriate to the lowest social classes in the areas where they lived. Skilled manual workers benefited somewhere in between these two extremes.

Currently the two most important aspects of planning and access to goods and services are the availability of physical access and the location of prosperity. Suburbanization and the lack of adequate investment in public transport have increased dependence on the private car for access to a wide range of urban facilities. The planning decisions that have contributed to this growing dependency have therefore increased the disadvantages suffered by those without their own private transport. This is a growing problem not only within the inner cities but also for groups such as the old, young and housewives who can become trapped in their poorly served ex-urban locations.

Finally and perhaps most importantly, Champion & Green (1988) have shown the strong correlation between prosperity and growth in a limited number of locations in Britain. This is leading to an increasing polarization of living standards. Much of the economic growth that has taken place during the 1980s has been confined to the South East and particularly to the western arc around London. Planning policies which have influenced the rise in land and house prices in these areas have contributed materially to the access of the higher paid service class to the opportunities in these areas and the exclusion of other groups or indeed anyone who cannot afford the price of accommodation in the South East.

Summary and conclusions

The effects of the British land-use planning system have been analyzed in terms of the nature and objectives of the system itself, urban containment, suburbanization, land and house prices, economic growth and residential segregation. In this section the results of these analyses will be summarized and some conclusions drawn.

First, the British planning system has to be seen as one based on conflict. At the core of these are conflicts between private property interests, which favour the use of markets to decide the uses to which they can put their property, and public interests, which look to public institutions, regulation and plans to provide goods and services which markets characteristically do not. There are also conflicts between different groups within these two large and general categories.

The outcomes of these conflicts rarely conform to the original intentions of all developers or public interests. One of the main divergences from the formal intentions of planning is the partial replacement of competitive markets in land and development with oligopolistic markets. In these modified circumstances a few large-scale developers come to dominate the markets in land and development where development is permitted by the planning system. This reduces competition in these local markets and is therefore unlikely to benefit the eventual consumers of development.

It is possible that this result suits both developers and the supporters of planning. This may be seen in the fact that the history of British planning is one of elite and paternalistic decisions to introduce effective public regulation over land-uses in the name of the public interest. When other interests were introduced into policy making for a relatively brief period during the 1970s, as a result of increased public participation, they were soon reduced in the face of economic problems. The 1980s saw the re-assertion of oligopolistic market forces over plans.

The re-assertion of oligopolistic market forces in planning brought to the fore the basic contradiction on which the whole enterprise rests. This is the conflict between the drive to assist large enterprises to maintain or increase their profits in the name of market forces by providing infrastructure, information and other enabling functions; and the need to legitimate planning to the general public by demonstrating that it also provides some benefits to them in the form of public participation, establishing social objectives and generally assisting to create social harmony.

It was possible to follow both these contradictory objectives during times of economic growth. But the first objective has taken precedence during the 1980s. This is partly because of economic limitations and partly because of the ideological predisposition of the Conservative central government. Nevertheless, the creation of oligopolistic markets in land and development by public action does not produce universal, public or mass benefits. This is shown by the analysis of the actual effects of the British planning system.

The first and most important intended effect of the British land-use planning system is that it has contained towns and cities. It has contained them in the sense that both physically and visually the growth of existing urban areas and the transfer of rural to urban land has been slowed dramatically and, in some cases, arrested altogether. Physical urban containment has stopped the outward expansion of cities, particularly in the belt running from London to Liverpool, around the point reached in 1938.

Despite this physical and visual containment cities such as London and Birmingham have continued to grow in functional terms. During the 1960s and 1970s processes of counter-urbanization or decentralized urbanization were at work. All the large conurbations lost both people and jobs. Highly selective streams of people and employment left the contained conurbations. They have become the inner urban cores of much larger functional cities. The problem for these core cities became not so much containment as how to avoid further decline.

Meanwhile, the policy of containment has forced these movements of people and jobs to cross Green Belts and to settle, along with other newcomers, in the next nearest towns beyond them. These have become increasingly important towns and cities in their own right. They represent a decentralized form of urbanism. In many respects they sap the new population and employment vitality of the central cores.

Those who could afford to make the move to the largely private sector labour and housing markets beyond the Green Belts have benefited from these changes. They have obtained housing in the areas where new employment opportunities have been growing, particularly in the South East.

Those who are contained within the disproportionately public or welfare sectors of housing and employment or unemployment in the inner cities are paying the price of containment. There they face the decline of traditional manual working-class employment and its replacement by non-manual service sector jobs. The better paid of these jobs are often taken by commuters from outside the urban cores. It is difficult for those who live in the public or private rented housing sectors to move house to more promising local labour market areas. This is because of the absolute lack of such accommodation in the developing areas and the impossibility of making exchanges between areas for residents of these kinds of property.

The policy of urban containment poses problems for those who can live outside the conurbations as well. Such suburbanization has led to the increasing separation of places of work from places of residence. This was not one of the original intentions of the post Second World War British planning system. The decentralization that was planned was intended to produce socially balanced and self-contained communities. The publicly planned new towns were supposed to exemplify these characteristics. In practice they did not turn out to fulfil these hopes. They were neither balanced nor did they prevent increasing commuting to other local labour market areas.

One reason why decentralized urbanization has been unbalanced and has contributed to increased traffic movements is that, although postwar population increase combined with rising incomes and car ownership made population decentralization inevitable, many urban local planning authorities were reluctant to see commercial activities go with them. Many commercial activities were kept in the older urban cores because the local authorities there perceived a need to sustain their tax base by maintaining commercial activities in those areas.

Often the local authorities themselves had rebuilt these centres after the war using 60-year Public Works Loan Board finance. Thus population decentralization combined with a reluctance on the part of urban local authorities to loose important parts of their tax bases also tended to increase traffic movements both for work and for major retail and distribution purposes.

Initially, much of this commuting was radial from small towns and rural areas to urban cores. It has been increasingly accomplished by private cars. In Britain these are often provided by employers and so those using them do not have to pay the financial costs of their journeys to work. The net results of these factors were early attempts to build radial and circular urban motorways to accommodate increases in traffic. These nearly always caused great disruption and, once built, proved to be inadequate.

Commuters on these radial journeys are faced with increasing congestion, delays and frustration in their journeys to work. Underinvestment in public transport makes this an equally frustrating alternative. Much of this scenario stems from the arrangement of land-uses arising from the policy of urban containment combined with inadequate public transport planning and investment.

More recently, however, movements between decentralized areas have been increasing. Thus as both jobs and people have left the cities peripheral and inter-suburban movements have increased. The M25 motorway around London is the most notorious example of an attempt to facilitate these types of journey. They are particularly difficult to accommodate using conventional kinds of public transport.

One of the major effects of containment policies is that they restrict the supply of land for development. Developers adjust to this effect by bidding up the price of land on which planning permission is forthcoming. Because this makes the land element in development more expensive developers are inclined to concentrate on the upper end of the housing market. Even there prices and densities are pushed up while the average size and quality of housing is reduced. Developers are able to make these changes because they are operating in less competitive, oligopolistic markets than was the case before statutory planning was introduced in 1947. They are also building less affordable housing because of the combination of planning constraints and less competitive market conditions.

Much of this is to expected from simple supply and demand theory. This states that restrictions in supply, other things being equal, will lead to increases in price. This is precisely what has happened with respect to the supply of development land which has been constrained by the planning system.

The result of constraints on the supply of land for development is that house prices are up to 40 per cent more than they would be without tough constraint policies. Houses are packed more densely on to smaller plots than they were before planning. They are also more often flats and terraced than detached or bungalows. The internal space standards of new houses do not reflect growing affluence and the need to accommodate more labour saving devices and leisure equipment. These are not the results that consumers would demand in competitive markets. In these circumstances they would require larger houses on larger plots.

These problems have been most acute in the South East. This is because of the concentration of economic activity and employment in that region. The South East contains nearly one third of the entire UK workforce. But the processes of counter-urbanization and decentralized urbanization have led to the situation where the majority of these jobs are no longer located in the metropolitan urban core which is Greater London. Instead, partly because of containment policies there, the majority are located outside London in the Rest of the South East. The concentration of employment there is so great that the ROSE on its own contains more employment than any other region in the UK.

The effects of containment on land prices and housing are so great that only large, consistent and long-term release of land would reduce house prices and improve their quality in Britain. This is also particularly true in the South East. Large-scale land releases need to take place in those regions or in local labour markets where housing demand is greatest. Releasing land in Yorkshire would have little effect on land and house prices in the South East.

Recognition of the scale of this problem has led to criticisms of Green

Belt policies in particular. The Regional Studies Association (1990), for example, published a detailed and informed critique of the policies in *Beyond Green Belts*. They list their faults as:

(a) Green Belts have restricted economic development in places and regions that need development.

(b) They have been a weak instrument of regional strategic planning.

(c) They have forced too much growth on towns and villages beyond the Green Belt.

(d) They have done little to improve the appearance of open land or promote the provision of recreation.

(e) Other policies have been as important as Green Belts in controlling urban development in the countryside.

While not advocating their complete abolition, they go on to argue that the policy is in need of a radical rethink. Among other objectives of any revisions should be the controlled release of much more land for development in regions such as the South East.

The case for the argument that planning retards economic growth has to rest mainly on the analysis of the effects of its direct costs on developers. This is because, although they may well be significant, nobody has yet managed to identify and measure the indirect and secondary costs of planning and their impact on rates of economic growth in other economic sectors.

The direct costs of planning on development are planning application fees, planning agreements and delays. Planning fees are insignificant for the largest developments and therefore have no measurable effect on them or their contribution to economic growth. Planning agreements can usually only be extracted in conditions of economic growth. This means that it is economic growth which determines the possibility of planning action rather than the other way around.

The greatest direct cost of planning which may retard economic growth is delay. This cost is felt most during property booms when growth in the development sector of the economy is at its periodic heights. Despite central government attempts to speed up planning decisions during the 1980s fewer applications for development were being processed within eight weeks towards the end of the decade than were at the beginning. This was partly due to the increase in numbers of

151

applications due to the property boom of the late 1980s. But it was also partly due to the level and detail of scrutiny considered necessary by LPAs. Changes in these areas still offer the potential for speeding up the planning system.

Many LPAs seem to spend too much time on trivial applications and arbitrary value judgements about design aesthetics. The results of all this effort tend to produce the lowest common denominator in design. They do not produce noticeably better results than a combination of expert computer systems and building control regulations would be able to achieve.

Despite this, the average time taken to progress from an application to a completed building on site has been reduced from around six years to three or four in some areas. This is as much a result of changes in the organization of construction as of procedural changes by planning authorities.

Planning delays and constraints placed on the release of land for development are the two major direct costs imposed by the British land-use planning system which are likely to retard economic growth. Their most serious effects are to absorb more investment in the development sector of the economy than would otherwise be the case. The extra cost of housing leaves households with less to spend on other items. This is illustrated by the lack of demand in the British economy during the current recession. Many analysts are arguing that recovery is dependent on housing markets picking up in order to revive demand in related sectors of the economy.

The last but not least effect of planning is to influence the distribution of scarce goods and services to different social classes, family and ethnic groups. Such differential distributions arise because of a complex set of relationships between where different social classes live, the facilities to which this gives them access and land-use planning decisions which influence those relationships. The evidence presented shows that, despite being imbued with the ideologies of community and social balance, planners have often produced quite opposite results in Britain.

The background to the effects which can be directly attributed to planning is that social change and polarization have been increasing in Britain. This is marked by increases in the service class, decreases in manual workers and increases in unemployment. This has been combined with increases in the residential segregation of these groups, particularly between prosperous and less prosperous areas. Those groups, such as ethnic minorities, have been trapped in the inner cities where they form a growing and disenchanted underclass.

The introduction of containment, suburbanization and increases in land prices by planning into these continuing changes has increased residential segregation and allocated better living environments to those who are already better off. This is particularly true of those suburbanites who live beyond the major cities in their Green Belts and the smaller towns and villages both in and beyond them. They have acquired the best housing, the highest capital gains and have been able to protect those gains for themselves by using the planning system.

The planning system has also influenced access to public goods and services. On the whole, planning decisions have improved the life chances of those for whom they are already highest. In contrast, those without cars and those who cannot afford house prices in the prosperous rural South East are excluded from access to the publicly provided goods and services there.

Many of the effects of British planning were not formally intended by the planners themselves. They have followed as the unintended consequences of policies such as urban containment. The paradox is that few of the major post-war reasons for constraining the supply of housing land are valid today.

The preservation of agricultural land for defence purposes is no longer necessary. The Common Agricultural Policy (CAP) of the European Community produces food surpluses on the one hand and pays farmers to "set aside" land from production altogether on the other. In such conditions there is a large surplus of land in Britain which is not needed for agricultural production.

The objections to pre-war urban sprawl were often voiced by design professionals in terms of its visual appearance rather than its functional provision of inexpensive housing for the masses. If anything, the alternative restricted estate developments that have been located away from the major cities are even worse in design terms, lacking in urban facilities and less affordable than their pre-war counterparts.

153

The decentralization of industry and commerce has taken place even with restrictive planning. It is no longer the dirty smoke-stack nuisance that was familiar before the war. It is increasingly high-technology based. The professionals who work in such new industry look for working environments which, among other things, improve the locality. This combined with the desperate need for economic growth of any kind argues for locational freedoms not provided within current policies of land-use constraint.

While this much has become increasingly obvious even in DoE sponsored research, there remains a political reluctance to alter the fundamentals of the British planning system as it has operated since 1947. This is true even after the detailed changes made to the system by the Conservative governments of the 1980s.

The question therefore arises as to what holds these basic fundamentals of the land-use planning system in place. The answer to this question lies in who makes the significant planning decisions and who benefits most from the operation of the system.

In highly centralized Britain, it is powerful individuals and groups who are able to use the existing social and political institutions, such as the planning system, to influence urban structure and the ways in which it is developed. Reade (1987) makes the pessimistic point that in any society in which land-use controls exist they will be "misused". This is because it is always difficult to say what the public interest in land-uses is and even more difficult to determine what combination or arrangement of them would actually be "best" in any circumstances. On the other hand it is much more possible for powerful groups such as the House Builders' Federation to discern what kinds of planning decisions would be in their own best interests. It is also possible for the high-income and well educated members of the service class to define and follow their interests in planning. It is much more difficult for the urban underclass to express "acceptable" demands and to negotiate them successfully with the British land-use planning system.

CHAPTER SEVEN

Planning at the crossroads: conclusions

Introduction

The three main themes of this book are pulled together in this conclud-ing chapter. They are discussed in relation to three questions. These questions are:

1 Why is planning at the crossroads?
2 Are the critiques of planning empirically valid?
3 Which direction should planning take next?

The answer to the first question revolves around the changes taking place in both West and East during the 1980s and 1990s. It is argued that, in the West, the combination of economic slump with the Reagan and Thatcher regimes exposed the underlying basis of planning and changed its nature and content on a permanent basis. In Eastern Eu-rope the collapse of their command economies and communism have put paid to the whole integrated public planning project in that area. This is also an experiment that is unlikely to be repeated.

The answer to the second question is that most of the critiques of planning are indeed empirically valid. They have been dismissed too lightly by planning apologists. The comparisons of the effects of land-use planning in California and Britain also tend to show that, other things being equal, the greater the degree of traditional planning regulation, the more valid are the criticisms of it.

Finally, some speculations on the future nature of planning are offered. These are based on the assumption that, from a planning point of view, it is necessary to meet and address at least some of the major criticisms. It may be, however, that what are seen as problems for planning are seen as benefits of the existing system by those interests who gain most from it.

Why is planning at the crossroads?

The guiding principles of the Californian planning system are the protection and enhancement of the rights of private property owners and limited intervention in development markets. Just as most public policies, it is a system responding to mutually incompatible, external conflicts of interest. In the case of planning these conflicts are between private versus public interests; private individuals versus public institutions; private property rights versus public regulation; and between markets and plans. These conflicts pull the system in different directions. The outcomes at any particular point in time depend upon the balance of forces in contention over particular issues.

Throughout much of the 1970s and 1980s California experienced economic and urban growth. Planning, however, reached a crossroads for two reasons. First, property owning households voted to restrict their local property based taxes and so limited the funds available to local government there. This led to a growing reliance by local governments on sales tax revenues and the so-called fiscalization of local planning. Secondly, a corollary of the fiscalization of local planning, local residents started to demand the management of urban growth in order to minimize the costs of new public services to existing residents.

The net result is that, in California, planning has changed from being a system primarily concerned with the spread of urban development, albeit in single-use zones, to a system which increasingly encourages high sales tax developments and slows down residential developments which would use public services.

In Britain, similar pressures have been brought to bear on the funding of local government and local services. Here, a combination of economic recession and depression with intellectual and political attacks on planning led to major changes in local authority funding and public planning practice. Many activities have been removed from public planning to markets, and the funds for local collective activities have been cut.

The net result of these changes in Britain is that planning has been changed in some respects to make permission for all kinds of development quicker and easier to obtain. On the other hand, unlike even those areas with growth management policies in California, the British planning system continues to operate tough containment policies in precisely those areas where economic and urban growth are most possible.

In both America and Britain the presumed effects of operating such land-use planning policies have led to important critiques of the activity. In Britain, selected elements of these critiques were taken up by the Thatcher administrations and resulted in major changes to the activity. More such changes are promised during the 1990s.

The responses by planning theorists and practitioners to these critiques and changes have either been non-existent or ineffective. Those who have responded have often sought a return to past practices. The argument here is that, particularly if there is any empirical validity in the critiques of planning, a return to past practices could not be justified. On the other hand, in lieu of a positive response by planners to these critiques, the profession will continue to be dragged along paths chosen for it by an apparently unsympathetic central government.

This brings British planning to its present crossroads. It can respond effectively to critiques of what it does and try to maintain some initiative in the debates for the profession. It can follow the dictates of central government and become at best a form of local technical administration or at worst an external contractual activity. It cannot do nothing and expect to be left alone during the 1990s.

There are six major criticisms of planning that have been examined empirically here. They are:

(a) The most important problem for cities is poverty. It has not been part of land-use planning's remit to address this problem but, unintentionally, planning actions have tended to make it worse.

(b) Planning interferes with the proper working of the market. Only markets and not planners can deal with the complexity of cities.

(c) Planning reduces economic growth, wealth creation, innovation and experiment.

(d) The strong relationship between planning and politics allows well organized pressure groups to use the planning system for their own ends.

(e) The values of planners often penalize the poorer classes.

(f) Planning imposes additional and unnecessary costs on development.

These criticisms are examined by comparing the effects of low levels of planning in California with those of higher levels in Britain. The most important of these follow from the degrees of urban containment imposed by the different planning systems. In order for the above criticisms to be shown to be both valid and the responsibility of planning rather than of other activities, their effects need to be shown to be most significant in the most planned circumstances of the South East of England and least significant in the least planned circumstances of the majority of cities in California, which still do not have planned growth management policies.

Are the critiques of planning empirically valid?

1 The first major criticism of planning is that the real problems of cities arise from poverty. This is beyond the scope and remit of land-use planning. Planners are therefore irrelevant to the solution of these problems and have actually made them worse by their interference.

The evidence from California and Britain is that, although it is usually true that poverty is beyond the statutory brief of land-use planning, nevertheless the activity has significant unintended consequences for urban poverty. This is because planning influences the distribution of scarce goods and services to different social classes, family and ethnic groups. Such differential distributions arise because of a complex set of relationships between where different social

158

classes live, the facilities to which this gives them access and land-use planning decisions which influence those relationships.

The basis of differential access to physical life chances is residential segregation. This is important because of the differences in access to a wide range of both public and private goods and services that follows where families are able to live. On the one hand some locations give access to clean environments, good schools, parks and other public and private benefits. Other locations trap those who cannot escape from them in unhealthy surroundings with minimal or non-existent public facilities. The arrangement of these locational differences and opportunities on the ground in terms of new land-uses and the built environment, has, in the past, been a prime official concern of planning.

In America, planning and zoning have combined with a discriminatory housing finance system and the lack of a significant public housing programme to spread different social and racial groups out over space. This has produced residential and social segregation. Its most extreme forms are racial segregation and the urban ghettos.

As far as planning is concerned, exclusionary zoning and growth management policies have served to segregate populations according to their different abilities to pay for housing in the market place. GMPs have tended to make housing relatively scarcer, more expensive and larger. All these factors make for increased residential and social segregation.

In Britain, tough containment policies have contributed to the fact that, until very recently, people have continued to leave the big cities in large numbers. But, as with most longer distance migrations, such movement has been economically and socially selective. With the exception of public authority new towns and peripheral estates, those moving out of the cities have been the economically better-off who could afford to buy their own homes.

These selective streams of migration have taken place against a background of increases in the service class, decreases in the numbers of manual workers and increases in unemployment. This has been combined with increases in the residential segregation of these groups, particularly between prosperous and less prosperous areas.

Those groups, such as ethnic minorities, have been trapped in the inner cities where they form a growing and disenchanted underclass.

The introduction of containment, followed by suburbanization and increases in land prices, by the British planning system into these continuing changes, has increased residential segregation and allocated better living environments to those who are already better off. This is particularly true of those suburbanites who live beyond the major cities in their Green Belts and the smaller towns and villages both in and beyond them. They have acquired the best housing, the highest capital gains and have been able to protect those gains for themselves by using the planning system.

The planning system has also influenced access to public goods and services. On the whole, planning decisions have improved the life chances of those for whom they are already highest. In contrast, those without cars and those who cannot afford house prices in the prosperous rural South East are excluded from access to the publicly provided goods and services there.

Despite physical and visual containment cities such as London and Birmingham have continued to grow in functional terms. During the 1960s and 1970s processes of counter-urbanization or decentralized urbanization were at work. All the large conurbations lost both people and jobs. Highly selective streams of people and employment left the contained conurbations. They have become the inner urban cores of a much larger functional cities. The problem for these core cities became not so much containment as how to avoid further decline.

Meanwhile, the policy of containment has forced these movements of people and jobs to cross Green Belts and to settle, along with other newcomers, in the next nearest towns beyond them. These have become increasingly important towns and cities in their own right. They represent a decentralized form of urbanism. In many respects they sap the new population and employment vitality of the central cores.

Those who could afford to make the move to the largely private sector labour and housing markets beyond the Green Belts have benefited from these changes. They have obtained housing in the areas where new employment opportunities have been growing particularly in the South East.

Those who are contained within the disproportionately public or welfare sectors of housing and employment or unemployment in the inner cities are paying the price of containment. There they face the decline of traditional manual working-class employment and its replacement by non-manual service sector jobs. The better paid of these jobs are often taken by commuters from outside the urban cores. It is difficult for those who live in the public or private rented housing sectors to move house to more promising local labour market areas. This is because of the absolute lack of such accommodation in the developing areas and the impossibility of making exchanges between areas for residents of these kinds of property.

Both the Californian and British land-use planning systems have had the unintended effect of making the problems of urban poverty worse. The spread of single-family housing in Californian suburbs combined with the rise of GMPs has increased residential and social segregation. The policy of strict containment in Britain has had the same effects. The geographic and social segregation of those living outside the Green Belts from those living within them is probably greater than the differences between contiguous urban cores and suburbs in California. In this respect the British planning system has probably done more unintended harm than its Californian counterpart.

The conclusion of this discussion is that the criticism that planning has made the problems of urban poverty worse rather than better is valid. The fact that this was an unintended consequence of policies designed to achieve quite different physical objectives does not invalidate the criticism.

2 The second main criticism of land-use planning is that it interferes with the proper working of the market. Markets and not planners are the only mechanisms that can deal with the complexities of cities.

This criticism is usually based on the unstated assumption that the markets in question are perfectly competitive. In other words, prices and decisions are based on the actions of numerous and informed producers and consumers. Something like these conditions may have pertained in pre-Second World War Britain and in post-Second World War California.

One major feature that distinguishes Federal and Californian planning policy from that in Britain is that there are no national or state policies for intervention in land markets by the containment of urban growth. In California there were no effective planning mechanisms which could have been used to contain urban growth before 1971, when state planning law was changed to require the co-ordination of general plans and zoning ordinances.

Attitudes towards and policies for local urban containment can be divided into two main periods. In the first period lasting until the 1970s, there was little support for containment. One result of this was that millions of Americans were able to purchase relatively inexpensive and reasonably sized, single-family housing in the growing suburbs. As far as individual property owners were concerned this was a major benefit of having little intervention in land markets and no general or effective policies for urban containment.

But when GMPs began to be introduced in the 1970s one of their main effects was not to replace the operation of the market but to make local property markets less competitive. Smaller numbers of larger firms come to dominate local housing markets. Thus the major planning principle of limited intervention in development markets does not result in the maintenance of competitive markets. Instead, it encourages the establishment of oligopolistic, that is to say small numbers of larger firms, domination of local housing markets. These are not competitive markets. They are marked by characteristics which suit the interests of a few larger development firms. The small builders who had contributed to the building of the post Second World War suburbs have given way increasingly to the large building firms.

The important point to appreciate here is that even mild GMPs interfere with the working of competitive markets but actually assist the development of non-contestable and closed, imperfectly competitive markets. This suits the interests of large, oligopolistic developers. It is clearly not in the interests of consumers.

In Britain there is no question that land-use planning has interfered more dramatically than its Californian counterpart in the workings of land markets since 1947. The first and most important intended effect of the British land-use planning system is that it has replaced the unfettered workings of land markets by containing towns and cities. It has contained them in the sense that both physically and visually the growth of existing urban areas and the transfer of rural to urban land has been slowed dramatically and, in some cases, arrested altogether. Physical urban containment has stopped the outward expansion of cities, particularly in the belt running from London to Liverpool, around the point reached in 1938.

One of the main effects of this in Britain has been the replacement of competitive markets in land and development with oligopolistic markets. In these modified circumstances a few large-scale developers come to dominate local markets in land and development where development is permitted by the planning system. This reduces competition in these local markets and is therefore unlikely to benefit the eventual consumers of development.

Another way in which British local planning authorities have interfered with markets and reduced competition is by building or maintaining commercial activities in the old urban cores. Many such activities were kept in the older urban cores because the local authorities there perceived a need to sustain their tax base by maintaining them or because they had borrowed money from the Public Works Loan Board over periods of up to 60 years to build them there.

On the other hand, there are many externality effects of private actions in cities which even competitive markets cannot ameliorate. These externality effects are those created unintentionally or beyond the control of prices in a given market. Air pollution, for example, is created as a by-product of profitable production and the use of internal combustion engines in vehicles. Free markets do not put prices on this pollution so it is likely to continue unless governments and planners step in on the basis of a plan to reduce or prevent it. There are a whole range of pure and impure public goods and services of this type which only public action by governments on the basis of plans can cure, supply or charge a price for.

163

In this area of concern, planning in California is currently tougher than in Britain. The Californian Environmental Quality Act extracts more public information on the subject than any equivalent legislation in Britain. Even the European requirement for environmental impact statements on large projects has been sidestepped in the case of the Channel Tunnel by introducing it into parliament as what is called a hybrid bill. This central government tactic has even avoided putting the proposals through the normal planning procedures.

Nevertheless, it is concluded that the criticism that planning interferes with the proper working of the market is only partially correct and needs more careful definition. While it is true that GMPs and containment interfere with the working of competitive markets they do not abolish the market altogether. Instead, they tend to replace competitive with non-competitive, oligopolistic local land markets.

Furthermore, it is not true that only competitive markets can deal with the complexity of cities. There is a whole category of externality effects with which they do not and cannot deal. While there have been suggestions to arrange markets in such a way as to charge for such externalities as air pollution, this still requires planned intervention. Left to their own devices, free markets do not deal with the collective public costs of privately produced externality effects.

3 The third main criticism of planning is that it has reduced wealth creation. This is a cost of planning that has to be borne by society. It is argued that a dynamic and prosperous city economy requires inefficiency in its structure and land-use and that the rational pursuit of order by planners and others will kill off the potential economic growth sector, innovation and experimentation.

In California, during the 1970s, support began to grow specifically for limiting rates of local urban growth. This is expressed in the form of local initiatives for growth management policies. The effects of such policies have usually been to reduce the rate of growth of suburban single-family housing. But, the fiscalization of planning in California has meant that they have not reduced the rate of growth of commercial properties which provide sales tax revenues to hard-pressed local governments.

In general, GMPs only reduce the rate of local peripheral urban growth. They do not fix permanent limits to this growth in the way that, for example, Green Belts do in Britain. They are, therefore, not policies for absolute containment but for slower growth than would otherwise have been the case. It is not to be expected, therefore, that they will have such marked effects as the absolute containment of cities in Britain resulting from the rigid application of Green Belt policies.

In Britain, tougher containment policies have probably reduced the rate of economic growth by more than the combined effects of local GMPs in California. Here, the imposition of planning controls has inhibited the spread of manufacturing industry into the suburbs and the countryside. The guardians of suburban and rural amenity have prevented this. Thus amenity has been traded off against economic growth. The numerical scale of this trade-off has not so far proved amenable to measurement.

Thus the criticism that planning reduces wealth creation is possibly valid with respect to its indirect effects on sectors outside construction and development. As these effects have not yet been measured the force of this part of the criticism is reduced. The effects of the direct imposition of GMPs, specifically designed to reduce urban growth and Green Belts, which attempt to prohibit it, have been measured and do reduce and relocate growth. With respect to these two policies the criticism of planning is valid and more so in Britain than in California.

4 The fourth major criticism of planning is of the strong relationships between planning and politics. This is said to provide the potential for various forms of corruption. It has also allowed some well organized pressure groups to use the planning system for their own particular ends.

In California, the protection and enhancement of the rights of private property owners and limited intervention in development markets are the guiding principles of the planning system. This is largely because private property owners and large-scale developers are the best equipped and organized to obtain these outcomes from the conflicts surrounding planning. Financial appraisal systems, zoning ordinances, GMPs and other policies have all been supported by existing and potential private property owners.

The British planning system is based on conflicts between the drive to assist large enterprises to maintain or increase their profits in the name of market forces by providing infrastructure, information and other enabling functions; and the need to legitimate planning to the general public by demonstrating that it also provides some benefits to them in the form of public participation, establishing social objectives and generally assisting to create social harmony.

It was possible to follow both these contradictory objectives during times of economic growth. But the first objective has taken precedence during the 1980s. This is partly because of economic limitations and partly because of the ideological predisposition of the Conservative central government. Nevertheless, the creation of oligopolistic markets in land and development by public action does not produce universal, public or mass benefits. This has been shown by the analysis of the actual effects of the British planning system.

What holds the fundamentals of the British land-use planning system in place is the ability of powerful individuals and groups to use the existing social and political institutions, such as the planning system, to influence urban structure and the ways in which it is developed. This is because it is always difficult to say what the public interest in land-uses is and even more difficult to determine what combination or arrangement of them would actually be "best" in any circumstances. On the other hand it is much more possible for powerful groups such as the House Builders' Federation to discern what kinds of planning decisions would be in their own best interests. It is also possible for the high income and well educated members of the service class to define and follow their interests in planning. It is much more difficult for the urban underclass to express "acceptable" demands and to negotiate them successfully with the British land-use planning system.

It has to be accepted that well organized pressure groups do use political influence to ensure that the planning systems in both California and Britain are used for their own ends. This has given rise to suggestions for formally distancing planning from politics which will be discussed below.

5   A fifth major criticism of planning is that planners impose their own values on communities. This is often done to the detriment of the poorer classes. Vague and meaningless concepts such as social equality, wealth distribution and environmental protection are used to impose these values and undermine private property rights.

The thrust of the argument and evidence presented here is that planners are not in a position to impose their values on communities on major issues. The evidence from California is that many of the more important planning policies, such as GMPs, have been imposed on the planners by ballots initiated by better-off electors.

In Britain, planners spend a disproportionate amount of time on trivial applications and arbitrary value judgements about design aesthetics. But there is not much evidence that they are able to impose their values on major issues.

There is not enough evidence that planners can impose their values on any communities in California or Britain to substantiate this major criticism. While it may have been the case that planning elites wielded considerable power over the nature of planning in post-Second World War Britain: this power has slipped from them during the 1970s and 1980s.

6   The sixth and final criticism of planning is that it has generated additional and damaging costs. The separation of home and work pushes up the time and cost of commuting. Delays in the planning process push up developers' costs. Restrictions in the supply of land cause higher land and house prices. All these costs are attached to the planning system as opposed to markets. There is more empirical evidence on these practical results of planning than for any of the other major criticisms.

As far as commuting is concerned, one of the main effects of planning has been suburbanization and the increasing separation of home and work. This leads directly to functionally inefficient commuting, particularly where commuters insist on using their, or more often their companies', cars. This has bred congestion and demands for urban motorways which have been so destructive particularly of working-class housing.

Suburbanization is a process that has taken place without much planning in America. During earlier periods of suburbanization in California the separation of white-collar jobs from home was probably reduced. During this period employers were moving work to where suitable workforces already lived. These early moves divorced the location of work and housing from the older public transport systems and so made a growing number of journeys to work dependent on the private motor car and the public freeway system.

The growing problems of suburbanization have come with the continued growth of employment in the suburbs combined with public intervention in the supply of housing as a result of growth management policies and Proposition 13. This has led to a lack of new and affordable houses in those suburban locations where employment has been growing.

It is very difficult to link multiple suburban job locations with other suburban housing locations using public transport. The result is growing freeway congestion, lengthening journeys to work and increasing air pollution. Los Angeles and the San Francisco Bay Area are prime examples of these problems.

In Britain containment and suburbanization have led to increasing separation of places of work from places of residence. This was not one of the original intentions of the post Second World War British planning system. The decentralization that was planned was intended to produce socially balanced and self-contained communities. The publicly planned new towns were supposed to exemplify these characteristics. In practice they did not turn out to fulfil these hopes. They were neither balanced nor did they prevent increasing commuting to other local labour market areas.

Population decentralization combined with a reluctance on the part of urban local authorities to lose important parts of their tax bases, by rebuilding and protecting their commercial centres, also tended to increase traffic movements both for work and for major retail and distribution purposes.

Initially, much of this commuting was radial from small towns and rural areas to urban cores. It has been increasingly accomplished by private cars. In Britain these are often provided by employers and so those using them do not have to pay the financial costs of their journeys to work. The net results of these factors were early attempts to build radial and circular urban motorways to accommodate increases in traffic. These nearly always caused great disruption and, once built, proved to be inadequate.

Commuters on these radial journeys are faced with increasing congestion, delays and frustration in their journeys to work. Under-investment in public transport makes this an equally frustrating alternative. Much of this results from the arrangement of land-uses arising from the policy of urban containment combined with inadequate public transport planning and investment.

More recently, however, movements between decentralized areas have been increasing. Thus as both jobs and people have left the cities peripheral and inter-suburban movements have increased. The M25 motorway around London is the most notorious example of these types of journey. They are particularly difficult to accommodate using conventional kinds of public transport.

The problems of congestion and environmental pollution are severe in both California and Britain. Much of this is a direct result of the failure to link land-use and transport planning in any effective way.

Planning has also imposed additional costs on development by delays and fees. In California these can be shown to have increased the costs of development. In so far as increases in costs slow economic growth, then the effects of these planning actions probably serve to reduce rates of local economic growth.

On the other hand, developers can overcome some of these costs by entering into development agreements. These seem to be an increasingly important way in which developers, and particularly large developers, can secure favourable planning treatment for their future developments. Assuming that they are not ruled unconstitutional by the courts, they appear to be a way of reducing the costs imposed on developers by planning. They may be working in the opposite direction to delays and impact fees in so far as they reduce medium and long-term costs for developers.

In Britain the direct costs of planning on development are planning application fees, planning agreements and delays. Planning fees are insignificant for the largest developments and therefore have no measurable effect on them or their contribution to economic growth. Planning agreements can usually only be extracted in conditions of economic growth. This means that it is economic growth that determines the possibility of planning action rather than vice versa.

The greatest direct cost of planning that may retard economic growth is delay. This cost is felt most during property booms when growth in the development sector of the economy is at its periodic heights. Despite central government attempts to speed up planning decisions during the 1980s fewer applications for development were being processed within eight weeks towards the end of the decade than were at the beginning. This was partly because of the increase in numbers of applications due to the property boom of the late 1980s. But it was also partly due to the level and detail of scrutiny that was considered necessary by LPAs.

Despite this, the average time taken to progress from an application to a completed building on site has been reduced from around six years to three or four in some areas. This is as much a result of changes in the organization of construction as of procedural changes by planning authorities.

The most significant extra cost imposed by planning is that urban land and therefore house prices have been increased by GMPs and containment. The increases in Britain have been much greater than in California.

In California the restrictions imposed on the supply of building land have been much less general or severe than they have in Britain. So far they have not led to significant increases in density or reductions in the size of houses.

In contrast, in Britain where containment has been both general and relatively severe, by concentrating all development on to a relatively restricted supply of urban land, the planning system effectively raised its price. Developers have adjusted to this effect by bidding up the price of land on which planning permission is forthcoming. Because this makes the land element in development more expensive developers are inclined to concentrate on the upper end of the housing market. Even there prices and densities are pushed up while the average size and quality of housing is reduced. Developers are able to make these changes because they are operating in less competitive, oligopolistic markets than was the case before statutory planning was introduced in 1947. They are also building less affordable housing because of the combination of planning constraints and less competitive market conditions.

The result of constraints on the supply of land for development is that house prices are up to 40 per cent more than they would be without tough constraint policies. Houses are packed more densely on to smaller plots than they were before planning. They are also more often flats and terraced than semi-detached or bungalows. The internal space standards of new houses do not reflect growing affluence and the need to accommodate more labour-saving devices and leisure equipment. These are not the results that consumers would demand in competitive markets. In these circumstances they would require bigger houses on bigger plots.

The effects of containment on land prices and housing in Britain are so great that only large, consistent and long-term release of land would reduce house prices and improve their quality.

This is also particularly true in the South East. Large-scale land releases need to take place in those regions or local labour markets where housing demand is greatest. Releasing land in Yorkshire would have little effect on land and house prices in the South East.

As far as new consumers or those who would like to move to the more prosperous local labour markets are concerned, the increases in house prices occasioned by planning are one of its most damaging effects. It is unlikely that any change can be made to these effects without a major change in the general policy of urban containment.

The comparison of conditions in California and Britain is most revealing in the case of urban land and housing prices. The comparative lack of urban containment policies in California means that far more families are housed in relatively large, single-family houses on sizeable plots than in Britain. There is considerable suppressed demand for similar housing in this country.

Which direction should planning take next?

Urban containment

Many of the valid criticisms of the British planning system arise from the tough and crude form of urban containment that has been adopted since 1947. Green Belts have been used not only to contain specific cities but also to influence attitudes to development in rural areas that have no special designation at all. While the policy has suited county interests and has been very simple to follow because it is such a crude device, the reasons for its introduction are no longer valid.

The preservation of agricultural land for defence purposes is no longer necessary. The Common Agricultural Policy (CAP) of the European Community produces food surpluses on the one hand and pays farmers to set aside land from production altogether on the other. In such conditions there is a large surplus of land in Britain which is not needed for agricultural production. Nobody except the relevant farmers gains any advantages from paying for set aside.

The objections to pre-war urban sprawl were often voiced by design professionals in terms of its visual appearance rather than its functional provision of inexpensive housing for the masses. If anything, the alternative restricted estate developments that have been located away from the major cities are even worse in design terms, lacking in urban facilities and less affordable than their pre-war counterparts.

The decentralization of industry and commerce has taken place even with restrictive planning. It is no longer the dirty smoke-stack nuisance that was familiar before the war. It is increasingly high-technology based. The professionals who work in such new industry look for working environments which, among other things, improve the locality. This combined with the desperate need for economic growth of any kind argues for locational freedoms which are not provided within current policies of land-use constraint.

There is so little justification for the continuation of urban containment using existing Green Belt policy that it should be abolished. It should be replaced with something more like the regional planning policies for Paris. There large scale growth is channelled in corridors. These are provided with modern transport and communication systems. New forms of innovative industrial and commercial activities such as the Scientific City and Disneyland are positively encouraged. The urban development is interspersed with large public parks and forests.

The planned provision of unlimited but structured growth would provide not only a new direction for planning but also meet some of the major criticisms of the activity as it is now. First, it would bring local areas of economic growth closer to those most in need of jobs. This would be achieved by not forcing them beyond Green Belts and by developing modern transportation systems to link core areas with high unemployment to peripheral areas with jobs.

Secondly, it would make positively enabling economic growth, wealth creation, innovation and experimentation primary objectives of the planning system. The development rather than the containment of large cities should be used to encourage these outcomes.

Finally, the abolition of Green Belts would also reduce the costs imposed on urban land prices, development and housing by the planning system. Only large-scale and long-term planned releases of land for development can achieve this end.

Markets and planning

One of the undesirable effects of planning is its contribution to the reduction of competitive and the encouragement of non-competitive markets. This contributes to the lack of affordable housing and the excessive price of housing in Britain. One way of encouraging more competition and smaller firms into the production of affordable housing would be to take small developments of up to five or so units out of the planning system altogether. Proposals of this scale selling below a certain price should be made permitted development and dealt with through building regulations.

Freeing development of this scale from the necessity to gain planning permission would have the added advantage of reducing the flow of relatively trivial applications which are currently processed by local planning authorities. Lest this should be regarded as a particularly radical procedure, it should be remembered that what used to be the jewel of the Adriatic, Dubrovnic, was originally developed entirely on the basis of some 45 building regulations.

Increasing the scale and scope of permitted development would also have the advantage of taking non-significant proposals out of the realm of local politics. Such development could be dealt with more expeditiously on the basis of clearly defined building regulations operated using "expert" computer systems. Such procedures would also introduce more consistency into decision making.

A significant increase in what qualifies as permitted development and therefore does not need planning permission would meet the major criticisms of planning. On the positive side it would help to concentrate professional planning activity on the more important developments and more strategic issues.

Planning and externalities

Even the most hostile critics of planning are agreed that it has an important rôle to play in relation to market externalities. These externality effects are those created unintentionally or beyond the control of prices in a given market. Many environmental problems fall into this category. Despite its origins in the early public health legislation, British planning has not been so concerned with environmental issues as its Californian counterpart. The growing European requirement for environmental impact assessments should change this.

Environmental externality effects, their assessment and prevention, should become a more important part of the planning remit. Instead of devoting too much time and resources to arbitrary value judgements on the aesthetic merits of house extensions and the like, the planning system should be conducting impact analyses of the effects of major new developments. Over time, this would build up knowledge on the effects of planning based on empirical monitoring. The present lack of such information is shown by how little of the information available on what planning does actually comes from local planning authorities.

Concluding remarks

This book has attempted to show that many of the all too lightly dismissed criticisms of British planning are justified by the available empirical evidence. The comparison with less planning activity in California was used to show not only what the effects of planning have been in Britain but also that more rigorous urban containment has led to more justification of the criticisms of the effects of planning.

It is argued that these criticisms will not go away of their own accord. Indeed, the central government has acted upon many of them during the 1980s and seems set to take further action during the 1990s. British planning is all too accustomed to reacting to events rather than taking pro-active measures before it is overtaken.

Three major changes to this stance have been proposed in these conclusions. These are, first, to abandon the sacred cow of Green Belts and replace them with positive strategic proposals for large-scale urban development, transport and communications and public open space. Secondly, to aim to enable competitive markets and affordable housing by greatly increasing the scope and nature of permitted development and transferring such control as is needed of such development to expert computer systems operated under building regulations. Finally, the positive rôle of planning with respect to externalities and the environment should be developed. This should develop the whole public health rôle of planning. It should also accommodate the growing European requirement to know and assess the impacts and effects of major developments.

REFERENCES

Entries entirely in **bold** are edited volumes of contributions referred to more than once.

Abels, P. L. 1989. Planning and zoning. See Haar & Kayden (1989), 122–53.

Adam Smith Institute 1983. *Omega Report; local government policy*. London: Adam Smith Institute.

Adams, J. S. 1987. *Housing America in the 1980s*. New York: Russell Sage Foundation.

Ambrose, P. 1986. *Whatever happened to planning?* London: Methuen.

Ambrose, P. & B. Colenutt 1975. *The property machine*. Harmondsworth, England: Penguin.

Atkinson, M. W., N. Kessel, J. B. Dalgaard 1975. The comparability of suicide rates. *British Journal of Psychiatry* **127**, 247–56.

Audit Commission 1992. *Building in quality: a study of development control*. London: HMSO.

Babcock, R. 1969. *The zoning game*. Madison/Milwaukee: University of Wisconsin Press.

Babcock, R. & C. Siemon 1980. *The Zoning Game revisited*. Madison/Milwaukee: University of Wisconsin Press.

Bajt, A. 1987. La propriété sociale en tant que propriété de tous et de chacun. *Revue d'Études Comparatives Est–Ouest* **11**, 41–72.

Balchin, P. N. & G. H. Bull 1987. *Regional and urban economics*. London: Harper & Row.

Ball, M., M. Harloe, M. Martens 1989. *Housing and social change in Europe and the USA*. London: Routledge.

Banfield, E. 1974. *Unheavenly city revisited*. Boston, Mass.: Little Brown.

Banham, R., P. Barker, P. Hall, C. Price 1969. Non-plan: an experiment in freedom. *New Society*, 20 March.

Begg, I. & G. C. Cameron 1987. *High technology location and the urban areas of Great Britain*. Discussion Paper 19, Department of Land Economy, University of Cambridge.

Best, R. H. 1981. *Land-use and living space*. London: Methuen.

Best, R. H. & M. Anderson 1984. Land-use structure and change in Britain, 1971 to 1981. *The Planner* **70**(11), 21–4.

Beveridge Report 1942. *Social insurance and allied services*. London: HMSO.

Bibby, P. R. & J. W. Sheperd 1990. *Rates of urbanization in England 1981–2001*. London: HMSO.

Bowers, J. K. & P. Cheshire 1983. *Agriculture, the countryside and land-use: an economic critique*. London: Methuen.

Brindley, T., Y. Rydin, G. Stoker 1989. *Remaking planning: the politics of urban change in the Thatcher years*. London: Unwin Hyman.

Brower, D., et al. (eds) 1989. *Understanding growth management*. Washington DC: The Urban Land Institute.

Bruton, M. & D. Nicholson 1987. *Local planning in practice*. London: Hutchinson.

Caldarovic, O. 1991. Socialist urbanization and social segregation. See Simmie & Dekleva (1991), 131–42.

Centre for Policy Studies 1980. *A bibliography of freedom*. London: Centre for Policy Studies.

Cambridge Economic Policy Review 1982. *Volume 8*. Aldershot: Gower.

Central Statistical Office 1991. *Regional trends*. London: HMSO.

Cervero, R. 1986. *Suburban gridlock*. New Brunswick: Centre for Urban Policy Studies.

Champion, A. G., A. E. Green, D. W. Owen, D. J. Ellin, M. G. Coombes 1987. *Changing places: Britain's economic and social complexion*. London: Edward Arnold.

Champion, A. G. & A. E. Green 1988. *In search of Britain's booming towns*. CURDS Discussion Paper 72, Centre for Urban and Regional Development Studies, University of Newcastle.

Checkoway, B. 1984. Large builders, Federal housing programs, and postwar suburbanization. See Tabb & Sawers (1984), 52–73.

Cheshire, P. & S. Sheppard 1989. British planning policy and access to housing: some empirical estimates. *Urban Studies* **26**, 469–85.

Clawson, M. & P. Hall 1973. *Planning and urban growth: an Anglo–American comparison*. Baltimore: Johns Hopkins University Press.

Coleman, A. 1977. Land-use planning: success or failure? *Architects Journal* **165**(3), 94–134.

Council for the Protection of Rural England 1992. *The lost land: land-use change in England 1945–1990*. London: Council for the Protection of Rural England.

Coyle, S. 1983. Palo Alto: a far cry from Euclid. *Stanford Environmental Law Annual* **4**, 83–103.

Cullingworth, J. B. 1988. *Town and country planning in Britain*, 10th edn. London: Unwin Hyman.

Curtis, S. & J. Mohan 1989. The geography of ill-health and health care. In *The North/South divide: regional change in Britain in the 1980s*, J. Lewis & A. Townsend (eds). London: Paul Chapman.

Dale, A. 1987. The effect of life-cycle on three dimensions of stratification. In *Rethinking the life cycle*, A. Bryman et al. (eds). London: Macmillan.

Danish, P. D. 1986. Boulder's self-examination. In *Growth management: keeping on target?*, D. Porter (ed.). Washington DC: Urban Land Institute.

Davidson, B. 1975. The effects of land speculation on the supply of housing in England and Wales. *Urban Studies* **12**, 91–9.

Davies, J. G. 1972. *The evangelistic bureaucrat: a study of a planning exercise in Newcastle upon Tyne*. London: Tavistock.

Deakin, E. 1989. Growth controls and growth management: a summary and review of empirical research. See Brower et al. (1989).

Delafons, J. 1990. *Development impact fees and other devices*. Monograph 40, Institute for Urban and Regional Development, University of California, Berkeley.

Denman, D. R. 1980. *Land in a free society*. London: Centre for Policy Studies.

Dennis, N. 1972. *Public participation and planners' blight*. London: Faber & Faber.

Department of the Environment 1983. Circular 22/83, *Town and Country Planning Act 1971: planning gain*. London: HMSO.

Department of the Environment 1985. *Lifting the burden* [White Paper]. London: HMSO.

Department of the Environment 1976. *The recent course of land and property prices and the factors underlying it*. London: HMSO.

Department of the Environment 1986. *Assessment of the employment effects of economic development projects funded under the Urban Programme*. London: HMSO.

Department of the Environment 1987. *An evaluation of the Enterprise Zone experiment*. London: HMSO.

Department of Trade and Industry 1985. *Burdens on business: report of a scrutiny of administrative and legislative requirements*. London: HMSO.

Department of the Environment 1988. *An evaluation of the Urban Development Grant Programme*. London: HMSO.

Docklands Consultative Committee 1988. *Urban development corporations: six years in London's Docklands*. London: Docklands Consultative Committee.

Dowall, D. E. 1984. *The suburban squeeze: land conversion and regulation in the San Francisco Bay Area*. Berkeley: University of California Press.

Dunleavy, P. 1981. *The politics of mass housing in Britain, 1945–1975: a study of corporate power and professional influence in the welfare state*. Oxford: Oxford University Press.

Economist Intelligence Unit 1975. *Housing land availability in the South East*. Report to Department of Environment.

Elkin, S. 1974. *Politics and land-use planning: the London experience*. Cambridge: Cambridge University Press.

Elson, M. J. 1986. *Green belts: conflict mediation in the urban fringe*. London: Heinemann.

Evans, A. W. 1988. *No room! No room! The costs of the British town and country planning system*. London: Institute of Economic Affairs.

Eve, G. & Department of Land Economy 1992. *The relationship between house prices and land supply*. DoE Planning Research Programme. London: HMSO.

Ferris, J. 1972. *Participation in urban planning: the Barnsbury case*. London: Bell.

Fielding, T. & S. Halford 1990. *Patterns and processes of urban change in the United Kingdom*. DoE Reviews of Urban Research. London: HMSO.

Fischel, W. A. 1985. *The economics of zoning laws: a property rights approach to American land-use controls*. Baltimore: Johns Hopkins University Press.

Forester, J. 1987. Anticipating implementation: normative practices in planning and policy analysis. In *Confronting values in policy analysis: the politics of criteria*, F. Fischer & J. Forester (eds). Newbury Park, California: Sage.

Forshaw, J. H. & P. Abercrombie 1943. *County of London Plan*. London: London County Council.

Fothergill, S., S. Monk, M. Perry 1987. *Property and industrial development*. London: Hutchinson.

Frieden, B. J. 1979. *The environmental protection hustle*. Cambridge, Mass.: MIT Press.

Friedman, M. 1962. *Capitalism and freedom*. Chicago: University of Chicago Press.

Friedman, M. & R. Friedman 1980. *Free to choose*. Harmondsworth, England: Penguin.

Fulton, W. 1989. Wheeling and dealing in California. *Planning*, November, 4–9.

Fulton, W. 1991. *Guide to California planning*. Point Arena, California: Solano Press.

Gans, H. J. 1967. *The Levittowners: ways of life and politics in a new suburban community*. London: Allen Lane.

Gantar, P. & S. Mandic 1991. Social consequences of housing provision: problems and perspectives. See Simmie & Dekleva (1991), 119–30.

Geddes, P. 1915. *Cities in evolution*. London: Benn.

Glickfeld, M. & N. Levine 1992. *Regional growth . . . local reaction: the enactment effects of local growth control and management measures in California*. Los Angeles: Lincoln Institute of Land Policy.

Goldthorpe, J., C. Llewellyn, C. Payne 1987. *Social mobility and class structure in modern Britain*. Oxford: Oxford University Press.

Golubovic, Z. 1991. Characteristics, limits and perspectives of self-government: a critical reassessment. See Simmie & Dekleva (1991), 17–32, 33–44.

Grigson, W. S. 1986. *House prices in perspective: a review of South East evidence*. London: SERPLAN.

Haar, C. & J. Kayden 1989. *Zoning and the American Dream*. Chicago: American Planning Association.

Habermas, J. 1984. *The theory of communicative action*. London: Polity Press.

Halcrow Fox and Associates / Birkbeck College, University of London 1986. *Investigating population change in small to medium-sized areas*. London: Department of the Environment.

Hall, P., M. Breheny, R. McQuaid, D. Hart 1987. *Western sunrise: the genesis and growth of Britain's major high tech corridor*. London: Allen & Unwin.

Hall, P. (ed.) 1981. *The inner city in context: the final report of the Social Science Research Council Inner Cities Working Party*. London: Heinemann.

Hall, P. 1988. *Cities of tomorrow*. Oxford: Basil Blackwell.

Hall, P., R. Thomas, H. Gracey, R. Drewett 1973. *The containment of urban England* [2 vols]. London: George Allen & Unwin.

Haney, C., C. Banks, P. Zimbardo 1973. A study of prisoners and guards in a simulated prison. In *Society and the social sciences: an introduction*, D. Potter et al. (eds). London: Routledge & Kegan Paul / Open University.

Hayden, D. 1984. *Redesigning the American Dream: the future of housing, work, and family life*. New York: Norton.

Healy, P. 1983. *Local plans in British land-use planning*. Oxford: Pergamon.

Healy, P. 1992. A planner's day: knowledge and action in communicative practice. *American Planning Association, Journal* (Winter), 9–20.

Healy, P., P. McNamara, M. Elson, A. Doak 1989. *Land-use planning and the mediation of urban change.* Cambridge: Cambridge University Press.

Holmans, A. 1990. *House prices: changes through time at national and subnational level.* London: Department of the Environment.

Hooper, A., P. Pinch, S. Rogers 1989. Land availability in the South East. In *Growth and change in a core region,* M. Breheny & P. Congdon (eds). London: Pion.

House of Commons Employment Committee 1988. *The employment effects of urban development corporations,* Third Report. London: HMSO.

Jackson, K. T. 1981. The spatial dimensions of social control: race, ethnicity and government housing policy in the United States 1918–1968. In B. M. Stave (ed.).

Jackson, K. T. 1985. *Crabgrass frontier: the suburbanization of the United States.* New York: Oxford University Press.

Jacobs, J. 1965. *The death and life of great American cities.* Harmondsworth, England: Penguin.

Jacobs, J. 1970. *The economy of cities.* London: Jonathan Cape.

Johnes, G. 1987. Regional policy and industrial strategy in the Welsh economy. *Regional Studies* 21(6), 555–67.

Jowell, J. 1977. Bargaining in development control. *Journal of Planning and Environmental Law* (July), 414–33.

Juelsgaard, J. 1983. Atherton: Applying the State's Fair Share Housing Requirements. *Stanford Environmental Law Annual* 4, 130–42.

Keating, D. W., K. P. Rasey, N. Krumholz 1990. Community development corporations in the United States: their rôle in housing and urban redevelopment. See van Vleit, W. (1990), 206–18.

Kingston, M. 1981. *Monitoring in town and country planning.* MTP thesis, University of Manchester.

Kovac, B. 1991. Entrepreneurship and privatization of social ownership in economic reforms. See Simmie & Dekleva (1991), 17–32, 87–100.

Landis, J. D. 1986. Land regulation and the price of new housing. *American Planning Association, Journal* (Winter), 9–21.

Lee, J. M., B. Wood, B. W. Solomon, P. Walters 1974. *The scope of local initiative: a study of Cheshire County Council.* London: Martin Robertson.

Magee, B. 1973. *Popper.* London: Collins.

Marshall, M. A. & R. L. Florida 1990. Economic restructuring and the changing rôle of the state in US housing. See van Vleit (1990), 31–46.

Mason, T. 1977. *Inner-city housing and renewal policy: a housing profile of Cheetham Hill, Manchester and Salford.* Research Series 23. London: Centre for Environmental Studies.

McAuslan, P. 1980. *The ideologies of planning law.* Oxford: Pergamon.

McNeill, P. & C. Townley 1986. *Fundamentals of sociology.* London: Hutchinson.

Mellor J. R. 1977. *Urban sociology in an urbanized society.* London: Routledge &

Kegan Paul.

Mencinger, J. 1991. From a capitalist to a capitalist economy? See Simmie & Dekleva (1991), 17–32, 71–86.

Milgram, S. 1965. Some conditions of obedience and disobedience to authority. *Human Relations* **18**, 57–74.

Miller, T. I. 1986. Must growth restrictions eliminate moderate-priced housing? *American Planning Association, Journal* (Summer), 319–25.

Mitchell, J. 1990. *Containment – breaking the mould: planning for housing in the South East and the potential contribution of new settlements*. MPhil thesis, University of London.

Moore, B., J. Rhodes, P. Tyler 1986. *The effects of government regional economic policy*. London: HMSO.

Mumford, L. 1938. *The culture of cities*. London: Secker & Warburg.

Nairn, I. 1965. *The American landscape: a critical view*. New York: Random House.

Newby, H. 1979. *Green and pleasant land? Social change in rural England*. Harmondsworth: Penguin.

Niebanck, P. L. 1989. Growth controls and the production of inequality. See Brower et al. (1989).

Nuffield Foundation 1986. *Town and country planning*. London: The Nuffield Foundation.

Pahl, R. E. 1965. *Urbs in rure*. Geographical Paper 2, Department of Geography, London School of Economics.

Pahl, R. 1970. *Whose city?* Harlow, England: Longman.

Paris, C. 1977. Birmingham: a study in urban renewal. *Centre for Environmental Studies Review* **1**, 54–61.

Paris. C. 1982. *Critical readings in planning theory*. Oxford: Pergamon.

Pearce, B., N. Curry, R. Goodchild 1978. *Land, planning and the market*. Occasional Paper 9, Department of Land Economy, University of Cambridge.

Peterson, A. L. 1989. The Takings Clause: in search of underlying principles. *California Law Review* **77**, 1299–363, 79–128.

Ratcliffe, J. 1974. *An introduction to town and country planning*. London: Hutchinson.

Reade, E. 1987. *British town and country planning*. Milton Keynes: Open University Press.

Regional Studies Association 1990. *Beyond green belts: managing urban growth in the 21st century*. London: Jessica Kingsley / Regional Studies Association.

Rex, J. & R. Moore 1967. *Race, community and conflict: a study of Sparkbrook*. London: Oxford University Press.

Royal Town Planning Institute (Southern Branch) 1989. *Planning achievements in southern England*. London: RTPI.

Rydin, Y. 1986. Residential development and the planning system. *Progress in Planning* **24**(1), 1–72.

Saunders, P. 1979. *Urban politics: a sociological interpretation*. London: Hutchinson.

Schwartz, S. I. & P. M. Zorn 1988. A critique of quasi-experimental and statistical controls for measuring program effects: application to urban growth control. *Journal of Policy Analysis and Management* 7, 491–505.

Schwartz, S. I., D. E. Hansen, R. Green 1984. The effect of growth control on the production of moderate-priced housing. *Land Economics* 60, 110–14.

Short, J. R. 1982. Urban policy and British cities. *American Planning Association, Journal* 48(1), 39–52.

Siegan, B. 1976. *Other people's property*. Lexington, Mass.: Lexington Books.

Siegan, B. 1972. *Land-use without zoning*. Lexington, Mass.: Lexington Books.

Sigg, E. 1985. California's Development Agreement statute. *Southwestern University Law Review* 15, 695–727.

Silver, H. 1990. Privatization, self-help, and public housing. See van Vleit (1990), 123–40.

Simmie, J. M. 1971. *Ideology and physical planning in Britain*. Town Planning Discussion Papers 16, Bartlett School of Architecture and Planning, University College London.

Simmie, J. M. 1974. *Citizens in conflict*. London: Hutchinson.

Simmie, J. M. 1981. *Power, property and corporatism: the political sociology of planning*. London: Macmillan.

Simmie, J. M. 1986. Structure plans, housing and political choice in the South East. *Catalyst* 2(2), 71–83.

Simmie J. M. & J. Dekleva 1991. *Yugoslavia in turmoil: after self-management*. London: Pinter.

Simmie, J. M., S. Olsberg, C. Tunnell 1992. Urban containment and land-use planning. *Land Use Policy* 9(1), 36–46.

Skeffington, A. M. 1969. *People and planning*. London: HMSO.

Smidovnik, J. 1991. Disfunctions of the system of self-management in the economy, in local territorial communities and in public administration. See Simmie & Dekleva (1991), 17–32.

Smith, B. 1988. California Development Agreements and British Planning Agreements: the struggle of the public land-use planner. *Town Planning Review* 59, 277–87.

Szelenyi, I. 1978. The relative autonomy of the state or state mode of production. Paper presented at a session of the Research Committee on the Sociology of Urban and Regional Development, 9th World Congress of Sociology, Uppsala, Sweden.

Tabb, W. K. & L. Sawers (eds) 1984. *Marxism and the metropolis: new perspectives in urban political economy*. New York: Oxford University Press.

Thornley, A. 1991. *Urban planning under Thatcherism: the challenge of the market*. London: Routledge.

Uthwatt 1942. *Final report of the Expert Committee on Compensation and Betterment*. London: HMSO.

van Vleit, W. (ed.) 1990. *Government and housing*. Beverly Hills: Sage.

Verlic-Dekleva, B. 1991. Implications of economic change to social policy. See Simmie & Dekleva (1991), 107–18.

von Hayek, F. A. 1944. *The road to serfdom*. London: Routledge & Kegan Paul.

von Hayek, F. A. 1960. *The constitution of liberty*. London: Routledge & Kegan Paul.

von Hayek, F. A. 1982 [first published in three vols: 1973, 1976, 1979]. *Law, legislation and liberty*. London: Routledge & Kegan Paul.

Walters, A. A., F. G. Pennance, W. A. West, D. R. Denman, B. Bracewell-Milnes, S. E. Denman, D. G. Slough, S. Ingram 1974. *Government and the land*. London: Institute of Economic Affairs.

Wood, M. 1982. *High Wycombe: the implementation of strategic planning policy in a restraint area in the South East*. Working Paper 67, Department of Town Planning, Oxford Polytechnic.

AUTHOR INDEX

SUBJECT INDEX